How I Found My Superpowers

An Introduction to the Spirit World

Katharine Branham

Copyright © 2021 by Katharine Branham

All rights reserved.

No portion of this book may be reproduced in any form without written permission from the publisher or author, except as permitted by U.S. copyright law.

Dedication

To God, the archangels, ascended masters, and light beings of the universe who guided me along my path.

Contents

	VI
	VII
Forword	VIII
Acknowledgments	XI
1. The Crab Boy	1
2. The Recital	14
3. The Palm Reader	31
4. The Cleated Angels	44
5. The Glow	59
6. The Leaving	79
7. The Glasses	99
8. The House	120
9. The Major	140
10. The Knowing	156
11. The Last Straw	172
12. About the Author	193

Yes. Wear the crown. Be the crown. You are the crown.
—*Miss Congeniality*, 2000

Every story in this memoir is true, but most names have been changed to protect the privacy of those concerned.

Trigger warning: this book contains descriptions of verbal, physical, and emotional child abuse.

Forword

Katharine Branham's entrance into my world not only created a change for the better, it also saved my life. Having experienced one of the most emotionally tragic events in existence—the loss of a child—I was at the beginning of the "Dark Night of the Soul." Of course, I didn't know it at the time. As if the loss of my son wasn't enough, I was drowning in a legal situation that was so out of character, I knew I had to be in the *Twilight Zone*. With everything going on in my life at the time, I seriously didn't want to exist.

Enter to the stage, one psychic medium, Katharine. Now, I must explain that I already had some experience with contacting psychics, though none of them seemed to have the fairytale crystal-ball abilities that we are fondly familiar with. In a last-ditch effort to gain some miraculous insight into my incorrigible life, I queried an online channel for psychic mediums. I clasped my hands in prayer and asked for the help of my deceased son, Alex. The page on the computer screen seemed to have a mind of its own and kept returning to one spot as I tried to scroll down. *What the hell is going on here?* I thought. As I became more aggravated at the uncontrollable computer screen, I realized that Katharine's photo kept popping up. I bellowed out to the empty space in my kitchen, "There's no way I'm going to call that chick—she's way too pretty." I certainly didn't want any unfiltered emotions to get in the way of my reading. As I continued looking, I couldn't shake the feeling that Alex was somehow leading me to call this pretty woman.

I finally acquiesced and called Katharine. After asking only my first name, she began to describe a young man in spirit who was with her. She described my son in such explicit detail that I had goosebumps from head to toe. I continued listening and just about lost control when she said, "He's telling me that his name is Alex, and you are his dad." Katharine continued giving me details and relaying information from Alex that only I knew. There was no way she could have known such specifics considering some of them Alex had taken to his grave. The call ended with amazement but curiosity just the same. The next several calls helped to mend a father's broken heart and led to a spiritual awakening I will never forget.

Over the course of the past seven years, I've been blessed to experience the dedication, resilience, and love of a true angel in disguise. Katharine Branham has brought inspiration and light to my life and to many others. She has worked professionally in the psychic and medical intuitive field for over a decade and has acquired thousands of clients. Many are high-profile celebrities and professionals, but she is unwavering in her client confidentiality and will not sacrifice her integrity for personal gain. I've never met such a trustworthy human being in my life.

Katharine's gifts are truly superpowers. She's an open-channel psychic and can see a person's life from conception to death through remote viewing. Her uncanny gifts allow her to experience what most people consider the supernatural or "behind the veil." I've read hundreds of books and spent countless hours researching the phenomena of the spirit world and metaphysics. I can tell you this for certain:

Katharine's ability to tap into the non-physical reality that exists beyond human sight is nothing short of extraordinary. When she sees an angel, archangel, ascended master, spirit, or ghost, the experience is the same as when the rest of us see each other. Her reach into other dimensional states of existence is far beyond the normal realm. She relies on her gifts of clairvoyance, clairaudience, and clairsentience to relay messages from deceased loved ones, spirit guides, and the "frequency" (God). Her messages and teachings continue to be appreciated by her followers on social media outlets. Countless praises continue flowing in daily from people around the world, giving thanks for Katharine's heartwarming advice and loving spirit. Honestly, I have tears running down my cheeks now as I consider the love and joy that she spreads to so many people.

Katharine wants everyone to realize that their individual experiences are lessons that can help lead them to a more heart-centered relationship with themselves, God, and all of humanity. Her main message in writing this book is to teach that everyone has their own superpowers and that their experiences are stepping-stones along the path to finding them.

This book shares Katharine's journey to finding her superpowers.

Of course, these abilities didn't come without a price. As you read her story, Katharine will take you down a journey of emotional pain and uncertainty as a child and the sharp confusion of a double-edged sword as an adult. This is not only her individual journey; this is humanity's journey. Each character in her story has a purpose and a lesson. Find out the role each one contributed to Katharine finding her superpowers. And find out how her story relates to your own journey in life. Take an adventure and find your own superpowers.

—

Major Austin Hart

Acknowledgments

If you were to look around my office, you would find stacks of notebooks that stand two to three feet in height. I've been taking notes for years on the incredible things I've learned and seen in the spirit world. There was never a real plan for the information; I didn't expect to write a book. I began keeping them when it occurred to me that my two children, Breezy and Zach, might want to have the notes so they could access the information if they needed or wanted it at some point in their lives. The frequency I mention throughout the book I came to know as God, the creator of all. As I look back, the strangest times were when God's frequency would wake me up in the night with explanations about things I had seen and would urge me to write those things down.

For years, I worked more than eight hours per day for days on end, without weekends off. I was so exhausted it was hard to pay attention to the things the frequency was teaching me. The frequency had been with me all along, yet it wasn't until adulthood that I realized God and the universe really had my back. Some of the experiences I endured were difficult while I was going through them because I didn't know that one day, I would see the shining light beyond the darkness. I want to thank the universe and God's love for guiding me through the years, even at times when there seemed to be no hope.

I'm grateful to my parents, who gave me the opportunity to incarnate during this time on Earth to help others. It was through the good times and bad that I learned to see and understand the spiritual world.

The motivation of never allowing myself to give up came with the blessing of my children. Breezy and Zach, I am so grateful that both of you chose me to be your mother during this lifetime.

I'm thankful for the incredible teachers I've met along the way, who might not even realize they helped when they did. They are mentioned throughout the chapters of this book. Some of the teachers I want to thank are Standing Eagle, Marty, C.J., Scarlett, Belinda Smart, Julie Snow, Veronica, and Utah Mike for their guidance, support, and love. All of these people have been an important part of my journey, and I am so grateful.

The number one person who is most important for me to mention and honor is Major Austin Hart. I would like to first thank him for his twenty-one years of service in the US Army, during which he not only went to war but raised two amazing children. It was his late son Alexander who led him to find me. The universe has a way of bringing the people one needs along their path at the right time. This book would not have been possible without Major Austin Hart's unwavering encouragement and his personal goal to get my information out into the world. With his help, I have a series of books coming out with all the teachings and information to aid humanity's awakening.

Chapter One

The Crab Boy

Trigger warning: this chapter contains descriptions of verbal, physical, and emotional child abuse.

"You are the biggest disappointment of my life" was a frequent phrase Mom would say to me. I was four. *How can I be a disappointment? What did I do?* were the constant questions on my mind. I didn't know what disappointment meant, but I knew it was bad. Sometimes when she would say it, she was practically spitting on me, so upset it looked as if she were about to explode.

Along with her cruel words, Mom would often decide to put me in "time out," which meant I would be shut in my closet where I'd have to stay for hours on end. The closet was exceptionally small, probably about two feet by two feet, with a piece of wood in the back that could slide up. When I would lift the panel, there were just pipes behind it. During times when I was in the closet, kind strangers would visit me. I didn't think much of it, as it was comforting to have them present, and I had no idea where they would come from or where they would go once they left. I just thought they lived behind that sliding panel.

There were a few times I opened it so I could peek in to see what was going on only to quickly close it, as I didn't want to bother them.

Sometimes I would sit and cry in the dark until I fell asleep. When I woke up, the door was slightly open, and I understood that meant I could come out. I would wander into the den, usually hungry, and Mom would be in the process of making dinner. There was nothing said to me about my time in the closet.

At that point, I only had one brother, and we were eleven months apart—most people thought we were twins. My mom was pregnant with my sister. Being so close in age, my brother and I would often get in fights, and Mom would tell my dad we were biting each other. One day, I heard her tell him she'd learned that the best way to handle kids who bite was to put a hot pepper in their mouth. She reached up to the top cabinet in the kitchen and pulled out a jar of tiny green peppers. She told my dad to grab me and hold me to the ground as she pulled one out and shoved it into my mouth. It didn't take much to keep me down—I was only four. I cried and screamed, choking on the pepper while my mouth was burning. Then she told my dad to hold my brother and do the same to him. The sad thing about it was that her energy field appeared happy and satisfied afterward.

On weeknights, when Dad came home from work, he would put his lunchbox down, greet Mom, then greet me. He would pet my hair, and I would go back to playing. Then, out of nowhere, Mom would get angry and tell me again how I was the biggest disappointment of her life. I didn't know what would occur between one moment and the next, but suddenly she would blow up.

I could always tell when Mom was angry by the color surrounding her. Her color would change when hate would well up in her energy field. She could be talking on the phone in a good mood, and as soon as she looked at me, her energy changed.

It was impossible to predict when my mom's anger would be triggered and when it wouldn't. I remember times when I was playing with my dolls and she would walk in to check on me. Instead of lashing out, she asked questions about my toys the way any other mother might. As nice as those calm moments were, I knew it was only a matter of time before her fury would flare again.

Soon, my younger sister was born, completing our family of three children. The years continued to roll by, and I don't think a week passed that I wasn't punished for something. I felt as though I didn't belong to the family at all.

We lived in a troubled area in Houston, and there were few things I had to look forward to, but one of them was visiting my cousins in Port Arthur, Texas. It was always fun; we would eat good food, and my aunts always knew how to make us feel welcome. My mom's sisters were very kind to us. They knew how to throw parties and made every event special. The only girl cousin I had was a few years older than me and would often have a box of clothes ready for Mom to go through to see what would fit me. I loved hand-me-down trips. I adored my cousin's clothes. Her mom was a seamstress and bought her beautiful outfits, so anything she had always looked great.

I don't know if my aunts knew quite how much I appreciated them, but I really did. I think they all knew deep down that something was going on from the physical appearance of my siblings and me. We were only bathed when it was necessary, so it wasn't a secret we weren't well cared for.

If it hadn't been for my aunts taking notice that I was covered in mosquito bites and untreated impetigo, I would have been in really bad shape. On one trip, my aunts noticed the impetigo had spread down my arm, and there was no way Mom would have taken me to the doctor had her sisters not told her to.

Despite my mother's failure to care for me, my parents were well-liked in the community. They'd met in high school. Mom enjoyed volunteering for things and was always joining organizations; she loved being with people and leading events. Everybody loved my dad—he was very handsome, and women went out of their way to talk to him.

All of us were baptized Greek Orthodox, but the closest Greek Orthodox church was thirty minutes away on Montrose Street, and unless it was a special occasion or a holiday, Mom and Dad didn't choose to make the drive.

One of my aunts had given me a small picture of Jesus in a little plastic frame about two inches square, and I would carry that around with me. When I got my Barbie house, I would put the picture of Jesus inside so the Barbies could see him.

After Mom had my little sister, she wanted some free time away from my brother and me, so she asked the neighbor's family to take us to church with them on Sundays. My neighbors were happy to do it; their son, not so much. Perhaps having us going into church with him was cramping his style. Dressed in our Sunday clothes, my brother and I would walk down the street to their house, and I would carry my little purse with my change for the offering plate. We attended a Church of the Nazarene with them until the family moved.

***

The year I turned seven is a year I will never forget. We spent sunup to sundown playing outside. Like most things in Texas, Texas mosquitoes are big. I'd have large, itchy bites up and down my legs, and scratching them would leave conspicuous welts. Not only were the bites noticeable, but I also felt ashamed about the way my legs looked after I would get hit with a belt by my parents or get injured in any way. After a punishment, I would look down at my legs to see if any marks could be seen.

I had lots of friends on the street to play with. We would usually jump rope, dance, or do each other's hair. There was a show we all loved to watch called *Soul Train*. Whenever we would play outside, we did our soul train dance down an aisle we would make by lining up, just like they did on the show. All the neighbors would sit outside and talk while watching the kids play. I think Mom got to the point where she didn't want to see me dancing in the street, possibly because some of the older girls had gotten in trouble for doing promiscuous acts between the houses. She certainly didn't want me outside anymore, so instead of allowing me to play, she enrolled me in dance class. One of the best things she'd ever done for me was deciding to put me in dance.

On my first day of class, I was scared and didn't want to go—until I put on the tights. They covered up my legs, and with the welts hidden, my legs were beautiful.

I didn't care too much for ballet, but I loved tap. I could really feel the beat. I loved the sound of the shoes on the floor. It brought me a new sense of calm and an escape from negative attention. I showed my dad my favorite tap step, the shuffle ball change. My hair was long, and I would wear it in a bun or ponytail when I danced. My dad loved my hair, and he would comment about how lovely it was. My hair was the one thing I thought was beautiful since my legs were always injured or covered in bites.

Mom was actually excited about my dance routines and recitals. One week before my recital, she said, "You need a hair trim."

I brushed her off and said, "No, I don't want it cut."

"It's just a trim. I'll only take off about an inch. You need to look good for your recital."

I sat down in the chair, not thinking much about it. She took the scissors and began cutting. Something felt odd, and as I reached my hand behind my head, I realized she had cut off all my hair. I looked down at the floor and saw the pile. Tears instantly ran out of my eyes as I looked at her. She didn't blink once; I could tell she was super happy. The color across her face was satisfaction. Mom's hair was always short. As I started screaming and crying harder, she said, "You kept moving. I had to cut it straight across to make it even."

Meanwhile, I was holding the hair that had dropped to the floor and sobbing. *Why, God?* I thought. *If you love me, why am I with a mother who hates me?*

Dad came in and greeted her. By that time, I think she was scared because she knew he would be mad. He looked at me, looked at her, and asked her to go into the bedroom. I knew he was angry and would say something to her.

She, of course, covered her tracks and said she didn't mean to cut it so short, but it needed to be evened out. My hair had always been long, to the middle of my back, and now it was cut all the way up to my ears. I knew Dad didn't believe her, and he, too, thought she cut it short on purpose.

I stood in front of the bathroom mirror staring at my reflection: I was scrawny, covered with infected mosquito bites, I had a rash on my arm that had to stay bandaged, and now my hair was cut to my ears. She had managed to take everything from me that could make me feel good about myself.

When I made it to dance class that week, the girls gathered around me, looking at my hair. I could tell the teacher and her assistant didn't like it. I was so ashamed of my appearance as my classmates touched my hair that I stood there and cried. Thankfully, I had friends, as it allowed me to witness normal households—or at least mothers who were not secretly trying to hurt their kids.

School was tough now that I had a bad haircut, but it kept people from noticing the cuts, bruises, and bites on my legs. I was bullied, and Mom didn't care. If she couldn't cause hurt, then, by all means, others could.

Don't get me wrong—there were some good times too, especially when we went out of town and visited our relatives, but for the most part, when Mom was reminded that I was there, she would say or do something to hurt me.

One of her favorite stories she told my dad and siblings was how I was playing in my room at fourteen months old. She walked in and checked on me to find that poo had fallen out of my diaper, and I had started to eat it. I never felt that was 100 percent true. She laughed so hard it was scary. I never told anyone that story.

***

After spring break that year, I noticed a new girl sitting alone at school. I sat down next to her, and we began talking. She didn't have anything to eat, and I asked if she planned to buy lunch. She said she didn't have any money and didn't have a lot of food at home. I took out my lunch, gave her half of my sandwich and chips, and shared my drink with her.

That went on for a week, then I was called in to see the principal. When I got to the office, my mom was sitting there. The principal said it was brought to his attention that I'd been sharing my lunch with another student. I told him she was a nice girl who had no food at home, and I knew she was hungry.

He said, "I didn't realize that was the case. I'll have someone look into it and will make sure she gets a meal every day."

When I went home that afternoon, I got the beating of my life. As Mom hit me, she said, "You're skinny; you need to eat." I told her there was enough for me just eating half a sandwich. That night, while I tried to get past the pain of my new injuries, I saw a man standing at the foot of my bed. He was dressed in a uniform of some sort that was tied with a belt at the waist. He didn't scare me. I actually felt calm. He didn't say a word, and I stared at him until I couldn't stay awake. The morning came, and it was the weekend.

My father and brother were in the backyard doing yard work. I was in my bedroom at the front of the house, playing with dolls. I heard Dad, thinking that he was coming in to get me to help him. I ran to the living room and hid behind a chair.

Mom was cleaning and looked up and said, "What are you doing?"

"I'm hiding from Dad," I said. "He's about to come in and ask me to help him with yard work."

"That's crazy—why would he ask you? That's men's work."

A minute later, my father walked in from the backyard, looked at her, and asked, "Where's Mary? I want her to help me with the yard."

My mom looked at him in shock, barely able to point to where I was before going off to her room. She didn't come out the rest of the day or night. She didn't come out the next day, either. She must've waited until we all went to sleep.

The following morning, I asked Dad if she would be out. He said, "She's dealing with a few things, and she's scared of you right now." At that moment, I began to wonder if Mom and Dad knew things people would say before they said them as I did.

He sat me down and explained that there was a time in history that if anybody did anything different from the norm, they would be called a witch and burned at the stake. I remember him explaining to me what it was like using examples from movies he had watched.

When he would say things like that, it would scare me and make me not want to share what I saw. I felt I was a weird child even when I was trying not to be. I didn't have the vocabulary to articulate my experiences and what made me different—I just knew I wasn't like everyone else.

***

While growing up, in addition to my many friends in the neighborhood, there was always a stray cat that needed love. I managed to get my parents on board with letting me keep and feed the cats.

I also began visiting other churches with friends since the family we'd been attending with had moved away. The Jesus at the church in my neighborhood was Black. The church a few neighborhoods over had a Latino Jesus, and in my aunt's church, he was light-skinned with blond-brown hair. I figured that which color Jesus was there for you depended on where you lived, just like Santa. Meanwhile, I still questioned why God would give me a mom who didn't want me if He loved me so.

There were times I wanted to ask an adult about some of the things happening in my family that I began to worry weren't normal, but I didn't have anyone who I was comfortable asking. I wondered if the way my mom punished me was typical, but then I remembered all the stories in my neighborhood about kids being pulled from their houses and having to go live with relatives because of something their parents did. Mom would make sure she told us how lucky we were to have her, and she would tell us the horrors of what neighbors were doing to their kids. Despite her attempts to convince us she was a good mother, her cruelty was all too real. I can't speak for my siblings, but there were nights I didn't think I would see morning.

***

My dad loved scary movies and anything on the Syfy channel. He would sit up and watch movies at night, and on rare occasions when I walked through the den to get a cup of water, I'd catch a glimpse of the screen, and he would explain the scene to me. If Mom caught me up talking to him, she would become angry, and I would pay for it the next day.

Dad's love of scary stories led to an intense experience in my young life. While I was in Camp Fire Girls, my brother was in Cub Scouts. My dad was a troop leader, and he had planned a trip to the USS *Lexington* in Corpus Christi, Texas. It was a Navy ship built in the 1940s, and rumor had it that it was haunted. As I've mentioned, Dad loved horror stories and science fiction. He thought it would be a fun trip for the boys and exciting for him. Mom, my sister, and I tagged along. Everything seemed fine getting there, but once we stepped on board that ship, I felt a real rush of nervousness as if there were lots of spirit beings around me—they weren't like my friends from the closet or the man who stood at the foot of my bed.

I turned to Mom and said, "I can't do this; I can't go on the ship."

"Oh, you're going to be fine," she said as she took me with one hand and my sister with the other and began walking us down the stairs and through the sleeping quarters. I could feel a cold energy pass across my back and down my arms, and every hair on my head was tingling.

Dad had mentioned that the ship was supposedly haunted. I believed it, but I didn't know anything about ghosts. Dad had a book in his bookcase titled *The Ghost I've Met*. I'd begun to wonder if my friends from the closet or the man at the foot of my bed were ghosts, but there was nothing scary about them, and they didn't have the same energy as what I was feeling on the ship. I began to cry. The sensitivity was way too much. I looked up at Mom and told her I needed to get off the boat. I could tell she relished the fact that I was squirming so much. She probably thought it was the most enjoyable passive-aggressive torture for me yet.

I couldn't shake the feeling of cold chills from the ship for several days after. The thought of those weird feelings coming from a ghost freaked me out further. *Could they have come home with me?* I wondered in fear. When we would visit carnivals, historical buildings, and even the Alamo, I had similar chills, but never so many at once.

For example, when we went to the carnival, there was a freakshow, and Dad wanted to see it. Mom refused to go into the exhibit and volunteered me with a push from the back. As I stumbled up, he said, "Okay, Mary, you are going in with me." He gripped the back of my neck while guiding me to the entrance. The outside of the exhibit was secluded and eerie. As I stepped into the tent, I felt a rush of emotions all at once. The main sentiment was fear, and it was not my own. I realized I was feeling the emotions of the people who were on display in the tent. The exhibition that brought on the most sadness was the star attraction, "Crab Boy." The outside of the exhibit had a giant sign of a cartoon-looking crab with a boy's face, smiling as he waved his claw. As I approached the pool in which Crab Boy sat, I was suddenly aware Dad's hand was still on the back of my neck. I'm sure anyone who saw us thought I was being forced to approach. Crab Boy and I locked eyes as I looked at him and he looked at me.

He was a boy with hands and feet that hadn't fully developed. He looked to be about four years old, wearing swim trunks while sitting in a shallow kiddie pool. The "Crab Boy" sign in front of him was one more reminder that he'd been stripped of his name and dignity for the crowd's passing entertainment. The pool was decorated with crab pictures on the outside.

I was so sad seeing the boy on display. I thought that with my differences, whatever they might be, Crab Boy and I could form our own group like the Super Friends. I felt sure people who had been alienated could support each other. His color showed he didn't want to be there. We had both been forced.

As we walked through the area, I asked Dad, "Why is Crab Boy here, and where is his family?"

He explained that when some people were born that way, the family would have them travel with the carnival to make money. I wished I could run back and rescue Crab Boy.

When we came out, Mom asked us to tell her what we saw. I didn't respond. She looked at me while eating kettle corn and said, "I think we should go see the fortune-teller."

I asked, "What's a fortune-teller?"

She laughed it off. I was still disturbed by seeing the sadness in Crab Boy. That evening, while riding in the car, my face lay pressed against the glass of the backseat window while I thought about him and wished for him to escape from the carnival so he could have a great life.

I saw the man in the belted uniform later that night. He would usually only be there when I was crying from punishments as I was going to sleep. The others had also started to visit even when I wasn't in the closet.

It was around that time I began getting a recurring dream of using a community bathroom where I sat down over a hole as a toilet. I mentioned the dream to my mom, and she said she'd never heard of anything like that and it was probably nothing. I knew it meant something and hoped to understand one day.

Chapter Two

The Recital

Dance classes were very helpful in building my confidence. At nine years old, I felt like I was ready to dance in a *Saturday Night Fever* kind of movie. Even though Mom and Dad wouldn't let me see the film, it was all anybody at the dance studio talked about. I could only listen in as the older girls were whispering about John Travolta's body. The one part of *Saturday Night Fever* I did see was the advertisement of John Travolta strutting his stuff down the street. I couldn't imagine a better scene. If I were in New York, I imagined I'd see guys walking like John, with the strut and all. I wondered what color was around John's beautiful body. It was probably yellow—that was the color of anyone happy. Who wouldn't be happy when they could dance like that? I knew there had to be other colors in John's energy field that no one else had.

On the day of my dance recital, I wore a powder-blue dress with split sleeves, a disco type of skirt, and a top with the word "dance" written in sequins and rhinestones across it. I felt incredible. My hair was long again, and no way was I falling for another haircut anytime soon. I could tell Mom thought I was beautiful too. When we walked into the Sam Houston Music Hall, people were commenting on my dress, and she was really proud—her energy showed she was in her element. That day she acted just like the other moms who were getting their children ready—putting makeup on me, carrying my clothes, and making sure everything was just right. I felt really special. I had my costume and my dance routine down, and Dad brought the camera to record the event. There was no volume, but it was still awesome that they cared to have a recording of that day. I wasn't as excited for my ballet, but for my tap routine, I knew I would shine.

After both of my performances, I changed back into the powder-blue dress and walked around backstage. They were asking us to begin lining up so when they called each of our names, we could go out and get our trophies. Mom was with me, and we could hear some commotion around the back door. There was a hysterical woman running around with a couple of other people. An older lady was standing there, explaining how the woman's little granddaughter from the "tiny tots" performance had wandered out the back door. The scary thing was that the door led to a very busy street in downtown Houston. I could understand why she was worried because when you opened the door, you could see cars passing by at a swift pace.

The older woman was tall, heavyset, and well-dressed—though I guess at my height, anybody would've seemed tall. The woman suddenly began to fall back, and I happened to be right behind her. I threw my arms out to catch her, but she collapsed onto the floor. I got knocked over as I missed being able to catch her and only slightly broke her fall. I was completely shaken. I got up, and everybody gathered around as I heard people yelling, "Call an ambulance! Call an ambulance!"

As I stood there still in shock, Mom grabbed my arm, telling me to shake it off. "You're about to go out and get your trophy. I don't want you to look like you've been crying—your dad's recording! You need to stop right now. Why are you so upset?"

"Mom, this woman just left," I answered.

"No, she didn't," she said. "Look, they're loading her up onto the stretcher right now, and they're taking her to the hospital. She's going to be fine."

While in tears and looking up to see where she might have vanished to, I said, "Mom, she's not fine; she left her body and isn't coming back."

As they rolled the grandmother out on the stretcher, Mom grabbed my arm and said, "Listen, she's going to the hospital—they're going to take care of her. She's going to be just fine. You've got to clean yourself up. Stop crying. Now get ready to go out there and get that trophy. Remember, your dad's recording."

It was at that moment I realized she didn't see the woman leave her body. I knew the woman who lay on the stretcher had no soul inside her anymore. I got an eerie feeling that I was the only one who witnessed her spirit leaving to join the light of God.

A woman came backstage, announcing for no one to panic; the little girl who had walked out the door came back and was with her mother. It seemed that someone stopped the little girl and walked her back in through the front door. She was completely safe. I was glad the little girl came back. The mother and little girl left for the hospital to see the grandmother. If they only knew the grandmother had already left. *I suppose they'll be told when they're at the hospital once the doctors realize they have the body without the soul*, I thought. My eyes were still red from crying, but I tried to pull myself together so I could go out and get my trophy.

On the ride home, I was exhausted. I fell asleep, and when I got back to my room, all I could do was step out of the dress and set the trophy down next to the bed. As I was going to sleep, I saw the man at the edge of the bed looking at me. After noticing him for years, I realized how comforting he had always been. He never scared me; I always felt like he was a good person just keeping an eye on me, and as I thought back, he only showed up on days that were really hard.

The next morning, I couldn't shake what had happened. Mom wouldn't ask about the woman, but I knew she had left to go to heaven. The soul that left looked just like her body, only transparent, and when she went up to heaven, she wasn't upset—she was okay. She actually seemed happy as if she knew where she was going.

When dance classes finally resumed, I inquired about the woman. It was clear from the look on my dance teacher's face she didn't want to tell me. She said the lady had many health issues and had gone to live with God. I knew when the lady left that she wasn't crying. I remembered how she instantly looked as if she knew where she wanted to go and was in no way hysterical about her granddaughter being missing anymore.

***

Later that summer, Mom signed me up for a dance convention that was coming to Houston: Art Stone's Dance Olympics. *Wow, dance Olympics!* I felt so grown up being dropped off at the convention room attached to a hotel. I ran through a mental checklist to make sure I brought everything I needed. *My favorite leotard and tights? Check. Dance bag? Check. Both tap and jazz shoes? Check.* I even brought a sack lunch for my break. It was time for Art Stone to make my dancing amazing.

As I walked in, the energy field of everyone there was yellow, which meant happiness. After having the experience of watching others be angry, happy, and everything in between, I knew yellow was happy, red or black was angry, and pink was love. I noticed one of my favorite student teachers from the studio, Lydia. I nervously waved at her from across the room.

She walked up and invited me to help look for her friends. She explained that a few groups of older kids had stayed at the hotel the night before rather than deal with Houston's morning traffic, and she wanted to make sure they were awake. As we were walking, she told me she was in love with Chad. He was the most handsome of the guys who took classes and taught at the studio. She wasn't the only one who would end up confessing to being in love with him.

When we found their rooms, we knocked on one of the doors. No one answered, but the door was partially open, so she pushed it wide and looked in. There were two large beds, and four of the guys were in one bed, cuddled together. When they heard us, they jumped up, wearing nothing. Once they realized how late they'd slept, they scurried around the room, grabbing their clothes and dance bags. I stood watching from the doorway, and with the curtains drawn, the only light in the room was a dim glow entering from the hall behind me. In the semi-darkness, I noticed the color around their bodies more than I ever had. Perhaps I had seen the colors, but the lights were so bright at the studio, I had missed the beauty.

As they threw dance clothes on, I could see that the colors around two of the guys were different from the others. Their energy field was a big pink ball that enveloped them both. I knew they loved each other. I watched them interact throughout the day and saw how their colors moved together. I had seen pink around other people before, but I found it so fascinating around those two because a single pink bubble enveloped them both, which was why I believed they loved each other. It was mutual—and one of the pink-enveloped lovers was Chad. That day while eating my sack lunch, I watched Lydia and Chad interact. She was acting like a person in love who had no idea she could never have him. I knew Lydia couldn't see colors around people, or she would've known it wasn't meant to be.

I began to notice colors around people more when I was with friends or just out and about. Later, the older kids at the studio came to know Chad was gay. I knew long before them because of what I'd seen at the dance camp—the pink bubble when he stood near Derek showed me their love. When the universe was teaching me something, it would be spotlighted by making the situation stand out, and in time, I would come to understand why.

I was sad that dance camp had ended. I had felt accepted by the older kids, maybe because I never mentioned things I saw them do, or maybe it was the fact that I was seen as the unpopular kid who they thought needed extra support. Thinking about it now, they were a beautiful group, the ones everyone wanted to dance like or look like, and then there was me. But it didn't matter to me what the reason was. I felt welcomed around them when they stood in their cliques before classes and warmed up to dance.

***

While I was lying in my bed one night, the light came through the blinds and shone on the little picture of Jesus in the plastic frame propped up in Barbie's house. Everyone had gone to bed. The house was silent, the road outside was silent—everything was silent except the stray dog barking along the opposite side of our fence. The barking was about forty feet away from my window. Our dog, Honey, was barking back at the stray. The stray had begun to make himself known every night over the previous week. The chain-link fence made it easy to see him running up and down, barking as if Honey were somewhere she wasn't supposed to be. I knew the dog would eventually get tired and go away like he usually did. I had seen the dog before but was unable to catch him. I think he would've been a good dog if he let someone who was kind get near him. While I was listening to the barking, all of a sudden, I heard a gunshot and then silence; not even Honey was barking. It wasn't uncommon to hear gunshots in our neighborhood, but I knew that one came from my parents' room.

I jumped out of bed and ran down the hallway to their room. I banged on the door, which they normally kept locked, and Mom answered. She was visibly shaken.

"What happened?" I asked her. My eyes took their own direction as I saw Dad leaning the shotgun back into the corner of the room where he kept it. He didn't say a word—he just got into bed.

I began to cry as Mom explained, "Your dad has to work in the morning, and he's so tired of that dog barking every night."

I glanced over at Dad. He didn't look at me, just looked at the ceiling. His energy was dark red, and all the edges of his energy field were black, with hooks pointed toward himself. I went back to bed crying; I lay there and thought about that stray dog and about the decision Dad had made to take its life. I knew Dad felt bad after, as there would not be hooks turned inward if he didn't. The hooks meant self-anger. I knew because I had seen them before when I felt I had done something wrong.

I knew he knew what he did was wrong. I had never seen anything like that in his energy field. There were times I had seen something similar in Mom's energy, but not quite to that extent. None of us ever mentioned that night again.

When I got to the dance studio the following week, I noticed Lydia with a few other older dancers sitting out front, talking to Chad's father. I walked up, and Chad's dad didn't say a word. Lydia looked at him and said, "It's okay. She never talks to anyone; she has known him for a couple of years and attended summer camp with us."

He smiled and began to explain that Chad was in some trouble. He wanted us all to write letters and put them in envelopes so he could give them to the judge. The letters needed to talk about Chad's character and what we had seen from him in the time we had known him. I sensed the situation was serious and nodded, agreeing to write the letter.

After Chad's father drove away, Lydia took me aside and explained that one of the girls from the junior class had needed a ride home. She was waiting out front, and they were locking up the studio. Chad had offered her a ride and dropped her off at her house. She was bragging to some friends about how she and Chad made out before he took her home. Those of us who attended summer camp knew he wasn't interested in girls, but nobody else at the studio knew. I didn't even think his family knew. It was really sad that he was facing false accusations. I knew how much Chad loved Derek from that pink bubble that enveloped both of them. In fact, it was one of those things I would never forget.

I felt guided to mention his love for Derek. I knew it was a secret, but I also felt like it would help him with his situation. That night I wrote a letter explaining that Chad was always kind, that kids his age would often overlook the younger ones and act like they were better, but Chad never did. He always tried to help everyone. Chad treated everyone with respect, and that was the best part of having him as a dance teacher. Then I talked about summer camp and how much Chad had influenced me because of his relationship with Derek. It was so inspiring to think one could find their true love doing what makes them happy. I explained that it was Chad who inspired me to start taking jazz.

All of us who were asked to write letters turned them over to Chad's sister so she could give them to the lawyer representing him. The following week, everyone was whispering about the girl who accused Chad and how the dance studio asked her not to come back. Chad had returned to teaching dance, and Derek was teaching too. The pink bubble in their energy field remained around them. The best part of the situation was that their relationship no longer needed to be kept a secret. I had learned for certain the pink bubble around two people meant love.

***

As I continued to notice more unusual things, I felt they were purposely being pointed out to me. Sometimes they were things like seeing the energy around a person or knowing what they were going to say. I felt that it wasn't appropriate for me to mention anything to anyone. *There has to be somebody who sees what I see*, I thought. I didn't imagine I was seeing things no one else saw. I knew most people reacted negatively when I shared my perceptions, yet I was sure others *must* have similar experiences. In moments when she seemed open to listening, I would try to explain to my mom that I sometimes knew what people were going to say. She would look at me as if I were weird—even weirder than I had been previously deemed.

Around that time, I mentioned the man I would see periodically standing at the end of my bed. I described what he was wearing: a military-looking suit with a belt. She ordered Dad to check my window to make sure it was locked. She arranged for me to go and tell someone exactly what I was seeing. That someone turned out to be a child psychologist. The psychologist told my mother it was completely normal for kids to think they see things or to have imaginary friends, but I knew the people I was seeing weren't imaginary. They showed up after each whipping and pepper night. The pepper nights became more infrequent as we were getting bigger; it was harder to hold us down while holding our mouths closed too. I think Mom also began to worry we might tell someone. The whippings became my parents' number one choice of punishment. Mom was also becoming more verbally abusive, and she seemed to exhaust all the ugly words she could link together. She used words that I didn't understand, and I rarely asked anyone what they meant.

One night was different. While Mom was watching TV with my siblings, I walked into the kitchen to get a cup of water. As I filled the cup and began to drink, I heard a voice frequency tell me to look up. As I did, I saw a man looking in through the window, and I screamed. This man was solid and in physical form, not like the one in my room.

Mom ran in and said, "What happened?"

As I was trying to speak, words were slow between breaths. I motioned to the window and said, "There was a man at the window, and he took off running."

She looked at me without missing a beat and said, "Of course he's looking in the window. You're dressed like a slut."

What's a slut? I thought.

I looked down at what I was wearing. It was an extra-large men's shirt my father had gotten free from the Ford dealership. It came down to my knees, was oversized, and covered everything. We would use the free tees as sleepshirts.

My father had been down the street talking to one of our neighbors, so Mom called and told him to come home. He came straight back, looked around the house, and didn't see anything. When he came inside, he locked up and asked what I had seen. I told him exactly what happened, and he said, "It's okay, there's nobody out there. We're safe."

I looked at him and said, "Dad, what's a slut?"

He got upset with me and asked, "Where did you hear that?"

"Mom called me that," I answered.

His color began to change. I thought about all the other names she had said to me over the years that I'd never asked about. I told him exactly what she said, and he patted my hair. "I don't know why she would say that to you." After he left, I got the feeling he felt sad for me and knew why she used that word.

If it weren't for the other things that I had going on in my life, such as dance, Camp Fire Girls, and our frequent trips to Port Arthur, I probably would not have survived that long. Whenever I was having a hard night, I thought about the stray dog and how I wished I could have saved him.

***

The Camp Fire Girls fundraiser was in full swing. I needed to sell candy for summer camp. I tried to do so in my neighborhood, but I could only talk to the folks my family knew; I wasn't allowed to go down certain streets at all. I knew I was going to sell the most, but how was I going to succeed when my perimeters were constricted? I told

Mom I knew I was going to be a top seller and win the giant stuffed fox. It was about five feet tall and three and a half feet wide. It was huge—the ultimate prize for whoever sold the most.

When the weekend came, Mom had Dad drive me out to Grammy's house. We loaded the Ford Pinto station wagon with nineteen cases of candy and nuts to take to her place. Grammy lived two hours away in Port Arthur, Texas, in a tiny house about three hundred square feet. She worked at a nightclub, checking people in at the door where she would stamp their hands so they could walk out to the parking lot and come back in if they wanted to. She set up a table right next to her stand where I could sell my candy. I was open for business. I had all nineteen cases stacked up, and I sat next to them, offering candy for sale as people entered the club. Occasionally, I'd walk to each table with a few products in hand to sell. I sold every box of candy and every jar of nuts that I brought that night.

Several of the men asked me to dance. *Dance, are you serious? Oh, I can dance.* I asked Grammy if it would be okay. She nodded and told me that they were safe. I had so much fun. I lived out my *Saturday Night Fever* fantasy right there in a smoke-filled nightclub in Port Arthur, Texas.

I loved visiting Grammy without Mom there. Grammy was Dad's mom, and I knew she loved me. Mom never gave her a chance, but I didn't understand why. When I visited, we would eat dinner at a two-top table, then I would get to take a bath in her ball-and-claw tub. I felt fancy. She would always style my hair, sometimes up. We'd end the night with *The Benny Hill Show*. She loved British humor, as she had lived in London. Her mother passed away when she was three, and she was raised by a wonderful stepmother who gave her a sister. They eventually left London for Bath, Maine. I loved seeing her laugh. We talked about the people I saw and how she just knew things about people too. I told her how Mom didn't understand, and Dad told me if I'd been alive at a different time, I would've been burned at the stake. I could tell by the look on her face she felt sadness for me but didn't know how to help. I think she feared if she said anything to my parents, they would no longer drive me over to visit.

Grammy told me stories of things she experienced. It was that night she told me about the legendary Colonel Buck's tomb and its curse. The story is that Colonel Buck burned a witch, and while she was burning, her leg rolled out of the fire. An image of the leg has appeared on his tombstone ever since. They have changed the tombstone out a few times, but the stain of the leg is still there. Grammy got up and went to a drawer where she pulled out a Polaroid of Colonel Buck's Tomb from her last visit to Maine. She handed it to me and said, "This is yours now."

I felt accepted—like she really got me. I asked her if she'd ever seen Jesus. She said no, but said she knew he was there. Despite Grammy's love, the same question continued to burden my heart. *If God's real, then why do I have a mom who doesn't like me?*

***

Mom's ability to organize events and her participation in committees made my friends in Camp Fire and school like her. She definitely knew how to throw a party. One year, she had a slumber party for my birthday. She made a Scooby-Doo-shaped cake. There were lots of games, and everyone was having a good time. As we were sitting around on our sleeping bags, Mom brought out a Ouija board.

"Where did the game come from?" I asked.

"It's not so much a game as a way to communicate with the spirits," she replied. "Now everybody gather around and place your fingertips on the ends of the disk that sits in the center."

I gingerly put my fingers on it. I didn't like what was happening; the whole thing gave me a weird feeling. The frequency that came across said, "Don't do it." I had a creepy feeling I couldn't shake. In fact, it was similar to how I felt when I had visited the USS *Lexington*. "Somebody turn on the lights," I declared loudly. It was beginning to feel like something was there. I glanced around but didn't know what I was looking for. *Something* felt like it was close, yet nothing could be seen.

The frequency I felt with the warning of "don't do it" made me realize I should never use the board again. I wasn't going to forget the sensation, as it felt like a clingy friend who was trying to stand right in front of my face. I wondered how many times Mom had used it. Was it something she had done on her own?

***

At that time, I attended the same elementary school I had for the previous three years. During the first week of fourth grade, the principal announced on the loudspeaker for the boys to go to the gym and the girls to the cafeteria. There was a girl who had started her period while wearing white pants, and kids were laughing and pointing. I had no idea what a period was until the counselor explained the menstrual cycle and said it was a natural part of growing up. She suggested that we go home and talk to our moms about any questions we had. Later that night, when Mom was in the kitchen cleaning, I went in and asked her questions to help me understand what the counselor had told us.

She became irate, and her energy field changed to pure hate. It looked as though her field were a huge black wave about to attack me.

"Mom! Why are you so mad? I just want to know if you can get pregnant from kissing."

She turned around and said, "I named you Mary after my mother, who was a kind and decent person. You are nothing like her."

That moment confirmed all my feelings of not being worthy—now I wasn't even worthy of my name. Mom looked at me with more anger than ever before and said, "I wish I could take the name Mary away from you." She was yelling at that point and said to get out of her face. "Just go! Go to your room and think about the person that you are."

I went to my room and cried, not knowing why I was born to that family. *Why would the counselor tell us to go ask our moms if it could result in this?* I wondered. I was lucky not to have been whipped for the question and grateful I could walk to my room and not be hobbling.

If I didn't deserve the name Mary, then I thought perhaps I should use my middle name, Katharine. That didn't seem to be attached to anybody Mom knew; she just liked the way it sounded together. Something felt off energetically about the whole situation with the name and Mom's outburst.

Of course, even after that night of her telling me how she wished she could take the name away from me, she continued to call me Mary, and every time she did, it felt like nails on a chalkboard. I knew she hated the fact she gave me the name, and whenever she would say it after that, I thought of that night.

Over the next few weeks, I began to pull away from the family, realizing there was just no way to make Mom happy. My friends and I would enjoy going to the roller rink. It was a lot of fun, and I earned money in various ways during the week so I could buy a ticket to go. I avoided talking to Mom altogether.

***

Our German neighbors who lived behind us had a chimpanzee named Grandpa. The fence was chain-link, so visiting with the neighbors was easy. Having that type of fence was fun because it gave a great view of Grandpa as he would swing on his playset, and I would swing on mine. Grandpa's energy was always a yellow and green mix.

One day while I was playing inside, Mom came in and said, "There's a woman talking to your dad through the fence. It must be a relative visiting the folks behind us. I want you to go outside and tell him I need him to come in."

I didn't want to stop playing Barbies, but I did as I was told. I felt I was earning brownie points with Mom. I walked out to the backyard, and I could see Dad wasn't watching the chimp as much as he was watching the blonde German beauty in the bikini. I told him Mom needed him to do something inside.

He said, "No, I'll be in later," as he casually laughed it off. "I'm out here talking," he said while looking directly at the bikini.

I went back in and reported exactly what he had told me. Mom said, "You go out, and you sit there. I want you to listen to what they're saying."

I went back out and sat down. I noticed the energetic exchange between them shift, and it felt like I was in a new space, yet still in the same space. Looking back, I realize it was a different dimension that I stepped into. I watched the two of them conversing back and forth and had no emotional connection to what was going on. The beautiful German had aggressive energy that was captivating and not like anything I had seen before. I zoned out as I began watching

Grandpa. Dad could have been making plans to move to Germany for all I knew. I was still trying to figure out what other people could see. *Can Grandpa see colors? I bet he can. I bet all animals do. Maybe I'm an animal, or at least part animal*, I thought. As I sat there at the fence while Dad talked to the beautiful German, I felt the frequency say, "This is why Mom doesn't like you; she sees you as a threat who took Dad's affection and attention from her." I wasn't able to understand. *Why?* I wondered.

***

I was rarely home, mainly staying the night at friends' houses. Mom encouraged me to stay away and was okay with me being gone altogether for days on end. During the times I was home, I tried to mind my own business, stay in my room, listen to music, sing, and play Barbies. I was on guard, careful not to set off Mom's anger. There were several things that would set her off, and I had noticed that asking why weird things happened was a big one.

One day when I was home and Dad and I talked, he worked into the conversation that he only stayed married for us kids. He said he thought of divorcing her often and was sad that she never had faith in him to do anything more than work every day. During that same conversation, I found out he had known I loved to dance, and when we couldn't afford for me to take dance classes, he worked out a deal with the studio to clean and strip their floors in exchange for my tuition every month. I thought about the times I would argue with him, as I felt he knew Mom didn't like me and had allowed me to suffer. I was getting older and started to understand he was in a tough situation and felt he couldn't leave.

Chapter Three

The Palm Reader

I began trying to form my own life by separating myself more from my family. When I was fifteen, I got my first job, and the added advantage outside of money was time away from the house. I focused on Wednesday night dance classes and going to the roller rink on weekends. Anytime Mom tried to talk to me, I completely tuned her out. It was so aggravating every time she would call me Mary. *If you regret the fact that you gave it to me, why are you using the name*? I wondered. I was very thankful that I had several friends from school and dance, so it made it easy for me to find other places to stay. I had friends I could stay with a few nights in a row because I knew she didn't want me home. I even slept over at their houses during school nights and would ride with them to school in the mornings. Many of them had parents who would pay us to do work around their homes.

I would shock my friends when I would tell them what someone was about to say. It would often happen when someone was about to suggest something I didn't want to do. I would lean over and tell the friend I was hanging out with what was about to be said. Michelle was usually the one I was relaying information to. She was so impressed.

I wasn't tuned in all the time but found myself more attuned the very moment someone would phrase a question. I was curious as to how often it happened to Michelle. I asked her if she ever knew what someone was about to say, and she laughed and said, "Never!"

It happened more often as I began to listen to the frequency before someone was about to speak. They thought I had some special trick to how I knew. I enjoyed the fact that Michelle thought it was cool. I still thought they could do it too, but they just weren't listening.

***

My on-again, off-again boyfriend, Ryan Schwartz, lived in River Oaks. The houses there were a block long. I didn't get to see him much since he lived far from me. I met him at the roller rink. We would make plans to meet at the rink for our dates. His mom, Lily, had my parents over for dinner so she could meet them. Lily was German and spoke German to Ryan when she wanted to say something she didn't want me to understand. I spent a lot of time with her, and sometimes she would let me look through her shoe collection and try them on. Before going out to dinner with Ryan and his family, I would bathe in her bathtub, which was sunken in the floor. There was a beautiful light that filled her room, and a Rembrandt hung over the sitting area. It was Lily who introduced me to Neiman Marcus, and when we would walk through the store, the staff would greet her. She wore a three-and-a-half-inch-long scorpion around her neck. Oddly enough, she and my mother shared the same zodiac sign of Scorpio. The piece was designed by one of Houston's finest jewelers. It had been on exhibit at a jewelers convention and contained many rubies and diamonds. It was set in such a way that when she moved, it was as if it were alive. The piece was probably worth more than the Rembrandt that hung in her room. Her energy was different than any I had seen. Lily had two boys and no girls, so I knew she liked it when people would mistake us as related. The trips to Neiman's made me want more and expanded my understanding of the real world outside the neighborhood in which I lived.

Ryan smelled of apple pectin shampoo and tanning lotion. He was very charming, but I could see other girls' energy in his energy field. I knew I couldn't trust him. I was beginning to notice that when someone lied, the color around their throat would change.

***

My new job was at a burger joint. I really disliked my uniform smelling like hamburgers every single day. It was almost as if the smell were embedded in every fiber of that uniform. To make matters worse, the fabric had a thick foamy polyester feeling about it.

My coworkers and I rotated checking the bathrooms, which also meant cleaning them. No one ever wanted to do it. There were two managers who worked there; one was a night manager, Christine, who worked evenings, and one was the day manager, Dan. One day, Dan was asking for a volunteer to clean the bathrooms. I heard a voice say, "Volunteer," as the frequency came through, so I held my hand up and said, "I'll do it." Everyone looked at me, shocked. I'd learned from experience that when I heard that frequency, it was something I should follow. There had been several times in the past when I heard the frequency telling me to do something or go a different way, and I had ignored it, then later wished I hadn't.

I went into the bathroom and began cleaning. I heard the frequency say, "Look down," and when I did, I noticed a diamond ring next to the toilet. I finished cleaning the bathroom, then walked up to Dan, showed him the ring, and told him I had found it in one of the stalls.

He looked at me in shock and said, "I will place this in the safe, and if someone doesn't come to claim it, it's yours."

The other employees standing around were muttering things about how they wouldn't have said anything if they had found it and how it was stupid to turn it in. Over the next two weeks, I forgot about the ring. When the time came, Dan approached me. He'd pulled the ring out from the safe and had it in his hand. "No one came in to claim it, so it's yours," he said as he handed it to me.

I enjoyed working. It gave me a chance to be away from the family and to have money to do things with my friends. My friend Tiffany worked there, too, manning the drive-thru. My job was simple: when someone would order a burger, I'd toss a patty down on the grill. There was a walk-in refrigerator with a small door on one side where workers could get slices of cheese and hamburger patties. There was a larger entrance around the back to access produce for slicing or for refilling the pickle container.

Tommy always worked the grill with me. He was a nice person, but he was a slob. His uniform could barely button, and his zipper was so worn that it was missing the little plastic teeth, so his underwear showed. His mannerisms were sloppy too. He was always spilling and dropping things without ever cleaning them up. One Friday evening, after the rush crowd had left, he went into the walk-in to refill our small pickle container on the prep stand. As he did, he spilled the monstrous pickle container that held mostly juice, with less than half of the contents being pickles. The strong odor was all we could smell every time we opened the small door to get a slice of cheese or a patty out. The pickle smell was beginning to get to me, which led to a discussion between Tommy and me.

As I was complaining to him, I noticed Christine walking from around the front counter with her hands up. There was a man behind her, and Christine said, "He has a gun; just do as you're told." The man told us to get inside the walk-in refrigerator, then he proceeded to close the door. There were seven of us working, so we were standing body to body in the small space. Once the door shut, the girls were crying. As I was trying to make a little extra room, I stepped back and slipped in the pickle juice. I fell against someone's legs, so I avoided hitting my head. My pants were completely drenched, and I began to cry from the cold discomfort of pickle juice and polyester mixed with my frustration at Tommy for not cleaning up his mess.

Tommy tried to bend down to pick me up. The other workers stepped onto the meat boxes to make room for him. Then we all heard his pants rip open. We all began to laugh when the door suddenly opened and a police officer was standing there. He asked us to come out and sit down so we could give him our version of what happened one by one in a separate booth, away from each other. When I sat down, he asked what I was doing right before we were all asked to go into the refrigerator. I explained the pickle juice spilling and how Tommy and I were arguing about why he should clean it up when my manager came around the counter with her hands up.

"So when did you see the gun?"

"Not right away," I explained. "It wasn't until he was closing the door that we saw the gun." I then thought about Christine's energy and how it didn't show fear; fear was a dark, orange-like color that was hard to miss around the body. It always showed when someone was scared.

I guess I paused for too long. The officer said, "Is there something you remember about what happened?"

In my mind, I pictured when Christine came around the corner—I didn't notice dark orange in her energy field. Even being scared myself, I would have seen the color. I told him, "Christine wasn't afraid."

"How do you know?"

I looked into his eyes and said, "I don't know how; I just know." After that, he told me I could leave.

Usually, when I would get home from work, I would bring home food left over from the shift. I walked in that night thinking about the events of the evening, and my family looked at me and said, "You reek of pickles. Did you bring home burgers?"

I explained that I didn't have any burgers and that we were robbed.

"Well, don't forget the food tomorrow night," they said.

"I don't think so; I'm not working tomorrow. I'm going to get another job," I told them.

When I got up the next day, I went to work to talk to the day manager. I explained that I didn't feel safe working there and that I appreciated him.

He looked at me and said, "If you know anyone who needs a job, we are looking for a new night manager. The police found out Christine was involved in the robbery."

***

The following Monday, one of my very best friends, Michelle, ran up to me in the hallway at school and showed me a Care Bear coloring book and a box of crayons. Michelle's color was bright yellow, and she had gold on the outer edges of her energy field. "We can color in class breaks or at lunch," she said. Michelle was adorable.

The Care Bears had names related to feelings, like Cheer Bear and Grumpy Bear. When I looked at the book, I noticed the bears' colors associated with their names didn't match up to what I perceived in people's energy fields when projecting those emotions. While we worked on the book, I asked if she saw color around a person when she looked at them. Michelle was confused by my question and eventually answered with a no, looking at me like I was being silly.

Michelle wanted me to go to the mall with her all the time, and she had an endless budget. She could buy anything she wanted, but you would never know just by looking at her. She always dressed super casual and had that '80s rocker style. She had all the cool things before anyone else did. Her dad, Frankie, owned a string of nightclubs and many other businesses in Houston. Frankie often offered Michelle and me odd jobs to make extra money. I made way more helping him than I did working at the burger place.

Michelle invited me over often. In fact, it was so often that her dad began treating me like one of his own children. Michelle's parents were divorced. Her mom was the true definition of a party girl. Michelle was one of three, and neither she nor her siblings ever saw their mom. Michelle was an amazing person and very generous like her dad.

Michelle lived across the street from Tiffany, who had worked at the burger place with me. She was one of two children and was being raised by a very strict Christian mother. They went to church every Sunday and had a hot meal at the table every day even though her mom worked. Her parents weren't together, but her dad had them over one weekend a month, and she felt loved by both of her parents. Tiffany dressed the best of any of us. She looked like the perfect sorority girl.

I spent a lot of time at both of their homes since Mom loved it when I stayed somewhere else. My neighborhood sat next to an area that was often mentioned on the evening news, and it was never in a good light. My friends accepted me but were afraid of my neighborhood, so they never asked to stay over.

On one particular day, I rode the bus home with Michelle and Tiffany, and we planned to watch MTV all night. As soon as we walked through the door of Michelle's house, Frankie said, "The couple who normally works the counter called out sick." He needed us to stand behind the counter at his laundromat and give out quarters to people who needed change. I was so excited to be able to hang out with my two best friends and make money at the same time. In fact, if it weren't for Frankie, I wouldn't have been able to go and do much of anything. Frankie gave us directions as I grabbed my Polaroid instant camera so I could take pictures while we worked.

When we arrived, the lady filling in didn't waste any time getting out of there. We took turns riding in the laundry baskets, racing each other in the open space. After taking several crazy pictures, we gave in to cleaning. Michelle was mopping, I was vacuuming lint from dryers, and Tiffany sat behind the counter. I noticed two very beautiful dark-haired ladies come in to load their laundry. After they loaded five machines, one walked to the counter and asked us where the usual workers were. Tiffany explained that we were filling in for them that night. She said, "Okay. They normally fluff and fold, and I pick up my laundry later. Would you be able to do that?"

"Sure, but we don't know what fluff and fold is," I said as I noticed a large sign hanging over the counter, listing it as an offered service.

The beautiful lady giggled and explained, "It's just loading the dryers and then folding and bagging the clothes to be picked up. I will pay the service fee plus sixty extra for you to split."

We agreed simultaneously. We maintained our word and were very conscientious about when the washer stopped. We quickly put everything into the dryer as we had promised. As soon as the dryer was finished, we began folding so that none of the laundry would have wrinkles. We still didn't know why it was called "fluff and fold," so we shook out the laundry before folding it properly. After folding everything nicely, we loaded the clothes into see-through bags and tied them tight so things wouldn't move around and shift. We hoped that when they got home, everything would still be folded properly.

Forty-five minutes after everything had been bagged, the ladies came back in, except they had two other ladies and three children with them. They looked related. Each woman was just as beautiful as the next, and the children were lovely and well-mannered. The one who had originally made the deal seemed impressed by our work as she turned the bags, looking at each one closely. She could see everything nicely stacked through the clear bags. I had even color-coded the items as I stacked them. One of the other women whispered to her, and the beautiful one leaned toward the counter, saying, "We would like to read your palms."

The shorter one standing next to her said, "We'll each read," while stepping forward and taking Michelle's hand. Michelle placed her palm upward, and the short beauty said to her, "You have always been rich and will always be rich. You will marry a wonderful man, and you will mother six children, none of whom you give birth to. You will have a very happy life." Michelle smiled and thanked her.

The long-lashed beauty stepped forward, asking Tiffany for her hand, and said, "You have been cared for and loved. You will make a series of bad decisions and finally learn some hard lessons and will be okay enough to get by."

The one who had asked us to do the fluff and fold moved over and put her hand out for mine. I turned my right palm up and placed it on her hand. I had never seen anything like that before and was in awe. She looked at me and said, "You have never had anything. One year from now, you're going to experience a very difficult time, and no one will be there for you."

"What about my dad?" I asked her.

She said, "He won't be able to be there for you. You will be married twice, but you will not feel they really love you. You will be in the public eye. You will have two children; you're going to help a lot of people and eventually write a book. You will not want for anything, as you will be very well-off." Then she reached into her purse, paid for the service, and laid down a one hundred dollar bill she told us to split. We were standing there amazed, and for the rest of the night, we talked about the palm readings from the beautiful ones. I was oblivious to the truth of the message, however, and soon forgot about what the woman had told me.

***

A year later and midway through my senior year, my dad came home after seeing a doctor. Mom called all of us kids together and said that the doctor told him he might have only two months to live. It didn't sink in, and I didn't know what to feel or think. I went to bed that night, but I didn't sleep. I was struggling in school that week, unable to pay attention. As I sat in history class, my eyes began to get sleepy, and the teacher walked up and slapped my desk with a book. "What's wrong with you—why aren't you paying attention in class? If you don't sit up straight and learn, you will fail, and then what kind of job will you have?" Turning to the class, she said, "You think history class doesn't matter?" She looked at me and said, "I'm going to give you an F for today, and it will be counted as a major grade."

At that moment, the thought in my mind was, *My dad is sick, and I'm sitting here listening to a woman teach things that are not one hundred percent true.* I stood up from my desk, picked up my notebook, left my textbook on the desk, and walked to the door. She got a crazy look on her face and exclaimed, "I'm going to take you to the principal's office."

"Don't bother. I'm not coming back to school," I told her.

I walked to the principal's office and told them I wanted to quit school. I explained to them that my dad was sick and I needed to go home. They called my mom because I wasn't eighteen yet, which meant I wasn't allowed to quit without a parent's consent.

"I can't make her stay in school," my mom said once she arrived at the office. "Her dad just found out he may only have two months to live."

The principal and the other people in the office tried to explain that if I were to leave school then, if I wanted to come back, I'd have to redo my whole senior year. My mom signed the papers anyway. Mom cried the whole way home because despite signing the papers, she still wasn't good with me being at the house all the time, so between tears, she urged me to continue staying at Michelle or Ryan's homes. I would come by the house to drive Dad to the doctor for his chemo treatments while Mom worked.

On one particular day, Ryan had loaned me one of his family's cars. It was a beautiful white Mercedes convertible with the gold package. I knew it would make Dad smile; he had taken us to many car, boat, and RV shows when we were younger, and he would fantasize about owning one. When I arrived, Dad was moving slowly but didn't want to seem unable to stand on his own, so he resisted help when he got into the car. I could tell he admired the beauty of the vehicle and enjoyed riding in it. We talked a little bit on the way to his appointment and on the way back. I stopped and got him a milkshake, hoping it would help put some weight on him because, within no time at all, he had become just skin and bones. When we pulled up in the driveway, we sat there and talked for a few minutes while sitting in the car. He told me he was concerned for my brother, sister, and me and wanted good things for us.

"Dad, we're going to be fine. You see the car we're in right now? I know I'm going to have this or better when I get older." I'll never forget the smile on his face. It was faint—as if he really wanted to believe me but couldn't see it happening. He ran his hands across the top of the dash while admiring the design. He got out and paused, taking one last look at the vehicle before closing the door. I helped him into the house and left.

When I got back to Ryan's, he said, "You're welcome to use any of the cars here." Ryan's family often traveled back and forth to Germany, exporting cars to the States. The garage had two Mercedes, three Porsches, and a Cadillac.

The next morning, Mom called me early and told me an ambulance was taking Dad to the hospital. I rushed down there to visit with him. He spoke to me privately, saying, "Please never let anyone talk you out of fulfilling your dreams." He moved his fingers to motion me to hold them. I held his hand, and he told me Ryan had asked for my hand in marriage, and after giving Ryan his blessing, he felt better about my future. I could tell by the light around his body he would be leaving soon. The visit was over, and that night I went to sleep crying as I thought of every good and sad memory.

The next morning I woke up to the phone ringing, and before I reached for it, I heard the frequency say, "That call is to tell you your father passed." I picked up the phone, and it was Mom, sobbing and telling me to come see her because Dad had passed.

Chapter Four

The Cleated Angels

I stood next to the car, wondering if it was all real, and looked up to the sky. The overcast was like something out of a vampire movie. As the haze of grief descended, Ryan came around, guided me into the seat, and closed the door. I was wondering where the man who used to stand at the foot of my bed had gone. I could use some comfort. The small plastic-framed Jesus picture was in my purse, and perhaps that would be enough to get me through the day.

My *theíos*, Nick—theíos means uncle in Greek—had helped guide Mom on arrangements for the funeral. She somehow turned to me for comfort. I guess in some way, she saw me as strong. During Dad's service, I stood next to her while my brother and sister stood back. I could tell by their eyes they had not been able to process the grief yet. Their connection to my parents was different from mine. I suspected that my brother and sister weren't aware Mom didn't want me around.

I was glad they had each other for comfort, though it had never felt good being the black sheep. I could feel Dad there and knew he was with Mom, but I couldn't tune in to him. I was at my lowest point, and I wondered, *If I'd been next to him when he left his body, would I have seen him go like I did the lady from the dance recital?*

The days after were tough. I could feel the energy shifts I had felt before, yet somehow, they were upgrading. When Lily heard that Ryan wanted to marry me, she took a private plane back to the States. She threatened to cut him off, as she wanted him to marry someone whose parents were rich like them. He told her he didn't care and was going to marry me anyway. I sat him down and told him that I'd learned a lot from him and our connection. At that moment, I knew by looking in his eyes he would never leave me unless I didn't want him. I told him there was another guy that I liked so he would go back to his family and do what they wanted of him. I knew what I had to do, but I still had a lot of sadness about my decision. I knew I couldn't love Ryan as a wife should, and I also knew he didn't know anything about being poor.

I thought about the characteristics of Scorpios as they had been laid out in the zodiac books that Mom had. I thought about how Mom and Lily were both Scorpios. It was so strange that I had experienced a Scorpio's sting from two different women in my life. The frequency came in and said, "You were too busy looking at them straight on and did not see the tail come up from behind."

During that time, I spent many days at the beach watching the ocean waves roll in. One afternoon as I sat on the sand, the frequency came in and said, "Remember the palm reader." I recalled the reading—how she mentioned that I would go through a tough time one year from that night and that my dad wouldn't be there for me. It had been a year, and I understood what she was talking about.

I sat, carefully recalling the other points she had mentioned when she looked at my palm and remembered she said I would be married twice. I quickly dismissed her, thinking of her foretelling the tough time—Dad's passing—as a coincidence. However, deep down, I knew it wasn't. As I ran my hand across the sand on the beach, I thought, *No one likes to be told they're going to be married twice.* Then I thought about Tiffany and how her reading was so bad nobody could imagine that being their path. *I suppose bad relationships are never planned.* I had heard through the grapevine that Tiffany was having a baby with a guy who had beaten her up. After sifting through the sand, I looked at my palm and the lines that ran across it. The frequency came again and said, "The palm reader didn't read the lines in your hand. She read the energy around your body." *The energy around the body?* I thought as I glanced at the couple walking toward me on the beach and looked at their energy. They had the love bubble around them like the one I saw around Chad and Derek from the dance studio.

During that time, I spent a lot of time alone. I worked at a mall doing perfume promotions for several department stores. As the customers would walk up and inquire about the fragrances, I would hand out samples. When I watched people shop, I noticed random markings in their energy fields. I didn't know why people had different markings but felt one day I would understand.

***

I went back to finish my degree that year but attended a different high school because we had moved. I was determined to make it a fun year.

Around that point in my life, there were several things I became certain of. One was the frequency. I knew it was real, even if no one else believed it was, but I needed to find out why I was the only one hearing the voice. I soon realized the frequency was the divine creator of the world, known as God—and I realized He *did* love me. I thought back to my childhood when I felt unimportant to Him, but at that point, I realized He had been preparing me all along. The question was, why me, and what was I being prepared for?

Mom was working and spending the rest of her days mourning. I could tell she needed me to be there for her. Dad had passed in the spring, and that would be our first Christmas without him. I felt like Mom needed something special that she wouldn't forget. I wanted her to be happy and hoped to find some way to make her feel better.

I was considered the new kid in school since most of the students knew each other from elementary. Several of the football players had tried to ask me out. I didn't pay attention to the guys who flirted with me, as I wanted to get through the year, gain my elusive diploma, and fulfill the promise I had made to my dad to finish school.

One day, I was pulling out of the parking lot and noticed several football players pointing and talking about me, so I pulled up and waved a few over. I told them I needed some help to lift my mom's spirits, explaining we'd lost my father in March and that he usually hung the Christmas lights. "I was wondering if any of you could come over and decorate the house." I told them I would order pizzas and we could have a Christmas light party. I thought only a few would show up, but over thirty boys came. I ordered thirty pizzas and soda, and I baked cookies while playing MTV loudly for those coming in and out to use the bathroom or grab a snack. I walked outside to make sure the cars and trucks of the players were not blocking the street when I noticed Mom pulling up from work. She got out of her car, and all she could do was smile. She waved and walked straight toward me while looking up at the roof to see the boys carefully stringing lights. Several of my friends also came over when they saw half the football team was at my house.

The energy field of those guys was more beautiful than any lights they hung that day. It was a golden-like color that emitted from the group as a whole. I'm sure they had no idea the full magnitude of what they did for us, but I've thought of them often with gratitude and love. They were our "cleated angels."

***

As spring approached, a friend of Mom's mentioned a singles group that met at a local Catholic church and suggested she attend. She declined the invitation until I told her I would go with her. I knew if I got her involved in a group, it would free me up. It was still hard being supportive of someone who hadn't wanted me around for years but now suddenly needed me.

I had my own stuff going on. My friend Maria liked a guy named Dillon, whose mom lived out in the country. We all agreed to go with Dillon for the weekend to see her. It was a very deserted area, and I could see no other houses or trailers around. Just to get to her house, we drove on an unpaved road for two miles. I would've had no idea where I was if someone had asked.

When we pulled up, his mother came running out to greet us. She looked like a goddess—a beautiful goddess. Her energy field was sparkly, and she glowed. She reached out, hugging and kissing Dillon while asking us to call her Marty, then reached for each one of us. As I hugged her, I noticed over her shoulder that a man was exiting the trailer who was not as eager to jump into the meet and greet. He waved and motioned from afar while saying, "Just call me Hank."

Marty invited us in and offered us lemonade and tea. I offered to help her with the drinks and walked into the kitchen with her. The sun was beginning to go down, and the breeze was lightly blowing through the trailer. Because of the time of day, the place was not well lit. I noticed her energy field even more than I had in the direct sunlight. She looked deep into me and asked about the ride out to see her. I could tell she wasn't listening to my response, only checking me out. I felt the frequency say, "She sees you." Then we joined the others in the den, and I passed out the drinks.

She sat on the floor and grabbed my hand, urging me to join her, then began to explain that she was an energy healing practitioner and wanted to clear my energy field. Dillon was slightly uncomfortable and tried to get her to stop talking about her interest. I lay on the floor, and she held her hands over my body. The others were talking about random things, and their voices began to fade out. I could feel the energy streaming from her hands, and I suddenly woke up with Maria and Marty peering over me. Maria looked worried, while Marty looked happy.

Maria asked, "How do you feel?"

"I feel great—like so much has been lifted off of me."

Marty commanded me to stand. "I need to rake your energy, and I want you to step outside so we can do it under the moonlight."

Maria asked again, "How are you feeling?" I could tell by the look on her face she was a little worried. Her dad was a sheriff and would tell her stories that left her paralyzed with fear. He was a great dad, and I knew he was just educating her on what happened out in the world. I couldn't resist messing with her and teased her by saying, "What could go wrong? You met a guy and agreed to let him drive seven of your friends out to see his mom in a location that no one is familiar with, only to find out it's the new location for a *Friday the 13th* movie." She got increasingly nervous, so I patted her on the back and told her I was feeling fantastic.

Maria then wanted to have a turn with Marty, so she lay there as Marty did her thing. The others had walked to the creek for some fish. The rest of the weekend was beautiful, and when it was over, I left there feeling better than I ever remembered feeling before. I went back to visit Marty another time with the same group, and she taught me so much about clearing the energy field. I was disappointed when Maria and Dillon broke up, as I had no way to see Marty again.

***

When I was twenty-one, I started working late nights at a high-end restaurant near the airport. I had my own apartment at that point. My off time was usually accounted for by running errands and getting reestablished for the week. I had agreed to go on a date with someone my friend Shannon set me up with. I had avoided dating for a while, but she insisted.

Shannon told me to meet him at the restaurant on the corner of Champions and 1960, and she gave me directions. When I pulled up, I noticed a small black kitten crouching down next to a car. I returned to my vehicle to grab a towel and went to pick up the kitten with it. It looked to be about two months old. I wrapped it in the towel and proceeded into the restaurant. My date was sitting in a booth, and as I approached, I noticed a couple staring at me. I introduced myself and told my date I had just found a kitten and needed to get it to the vet. Its ear and the side of its face were bleeding. "It must have gotten caught up in someone's engine," I explained.

The couple who had watched me walk to the booth leaned over to get my attention. They introduced themselves and told me the man was a vet. He'd overheard me say I'd just found the kitten out in the parking lot. Explaining that he was unavailable that evening, he handed me his name and directions on a napkin and said he would be glad to take a look at her on Monday at no charge. Based on her injuries, he said she should be fine until then.

I thanked him and his wife, then excused myself from the table, telling my date that maybe we could have dinner some other time. I needed to go to the pet store to get some food for the kitten. He suggested we skip dinner and go get the kitten food together.

I thought I should give the kitten a name, so I named her Alexis after Alexis Carrington from *Dynasty*. I called her Lexi for short. When Monday came around, I loaded Lexi up into the carrier and went over to see the vet. The office was silent, and no one was at the counter. I sat down and waited. The place felt eerie as if no one were there, then the door opened from the hall, and out walked a guy who looked like he had cried for days. His face was pale, and his eyes swollen and red. I think I startled him because when he looked up and saw me with the kitty carrier, he looked puzzled. "May I help you?"

I explained the whole situation to him and told him that the veterinarian had told me to come back that morning.

"Dr. and Mrs. Kingston died in a helicopter crash on Sunday morning."

I expressed my condolences to the man and asked, "How long did you work for him?"

"Long enough to know he loved animals and people. If you need a vet, there is one up the road about three miles on the right."

I got back into the car, and I headed in the direction of the new vet. When I got there, the lady who greeted me at the counter happened to be the veterinarian. She took a look at Lexi and told me she was going to need some skin grafts.

I inquired, "How much are your skin grafts?"

"Did you find the kitten?"

I told her the story about the restaurant and the vet, then asked what I could do. She said, "I'd be willing to give you a discount, but I'd have to charge you for the anesthesia supplies and the tech time."

"How much will that be?" I inquired.

"It's probably going to be around three hundred and eighty dollars," she said.

I told her I didn't have that kind of money and I'd try to figure something out. I left the kitten with her so it could get its shots and get treatment. By the color in the vet's energy field, I could tell she didn't have very many clients. I got into the car and was thinking about how I was going to come up with the money for the little kitten's vet bill when I remembered the ring that I had found in the restroom when I worked at the burger place. I'd placed it in a little box where I kept treasures I had found. One of the employees had told me the ring would be valuable. I went back home, picked up the ring, and headed to a pawn shop.

When I walked in, the energy was sad; I could feel tears from items people had lost. I stood at the counter, and when the guy walked up, I pulled the ring out and asked him how much I could get for it. He held it in his hand and put it under a lens mounted to the counter. As he turned it over, he dropped a liquid onto the metal, then wiped it off and said, "I can only give you four hundred and sixty dollars for it." I accepted the deal.

I went back home, got ready for work, and waited for the vet to call, thinking about how God brought the ring to me when I cleaned the restroom. So many things had been placed in my path that I didn't understand at the moment, only to discover later they were puzzle pieces that I needed.

Finally, I called the vet, and she said Lexi was doing well and would have surgery in the morning to see if they could do a skin graft for the part they couldn't do stitches on. When I went in the next afternoon to pick her up, they got the paperwork together showing proof of all her vaccines. The girl at the counter said, "The vet will be right out to talk to you."

When the vet came out, she explained that the bill was going to be a little bit more than what she had quoted. She showed me a piece of paper with the tally. I felt the frequency say, "She thinks you have a parent you can get money from." I tuned out her voice as I listened to the frequency, and as I tuned back into her voice, I heard her finish by saying, "...so that's why the amount is six hundred and forty."

"Six hundred and forty?!" I turned to her and said, "I live alone. I don't have six hundred and forty dollars. I just pawned a ring and got four hundred and sixty for it. You told me it was only going to be three eighty. You can either accept the four sixty I have, or you can keep the kitten." I knew she wouldn't keep Lexi, and I knew it would still be profitable for her to accept the offer. She looked at me, and I knew she was sizing me up on my threat to walk away. What she didn't know was that I knew what she was thinking. She glanced at the girl behind the counter and said, "Okay, I'll accept the four hundred and sixty dollars." I thanked her. She explained Lexi's aftercare and that she may need more skin grafts.

When I pulled back up to the apartment, I was excited to have Lexi home, but I must've left the lights on in the car because the next day, it wouldn't start. A guy coming out of his apartment offered to give me a jump. He got it going, and I was able to leave for work. The next day while I was coming into the complex, I noticed the same guy talking to a Native American man. I waved at him, and they walked over. He introduced his friend as Standing Eagle. He explained that his friend was Native American and that he'd taught him so much about herbs and medicine as they'd worked together doing their jobs. Standing Eagle told me he lived on land where a haunted house was open at Halloween and where he sold fireworks during "firecracker season." They explained that their boss allowed Standing Eagle to sleep on the land in his teepee.

I felt an urgency to tell him about Lexi, so I explained that I had found a kitten. She'd gone through treatments at the vet, but there was one patch of her skin that was not covered, and no skin graft was working. I asked if there was anything he could do for her. He told me to come by in a few days and he would make something up for me to use. The next couple of days went by quickly. I loaded Lexi's carrier and drove over to the old haunted house off of the interstate. When I got there, just like they had explained, I saw a teepee. Next to the teepee, there was a brand-new Mercedes with a giant bow. The Mercedes was covered in dust as if it had been driven there and just left.

I parked the car, took Lexi out of the carrier, and proceeded toward the teepee. I could hear some chanting, and as I peeked in, I saw Standing Eagle sewing. There was nothing for me to knock on, so I said, "Hello, excuse me."

He graciously invited me in and told me to have a seat. He set aside his sewing and reached for Lexi. He examined her, then handed her back to me. He turned and opened a couple of pouches. From one pouch, he took a couple of pinches and added them to a small leather bag, then he added a pinch from the other pouch. He strung the small leather bag and knotted it. He told me to wear it around my neck and to use the herbs on Lexi. I asked him what he was working on, and he told me that he was sewing beads on his bride's gown. He said it was tradition for the man to make the wedding gown. I asked him what his bride's name was, and he said he hadn't found one yet.

After we chatted, I put my shoes on and stood up outside the teepee. He got out of the teepee too, and when he did, I asked him about the car that was sitting out front. He said a woman had given it to him as a thank you.

"Thank you for what?" I asked.

He said he had met her son when he came to buy fireworks. The boy appeared to be a middle-schooler. Standing Eagle talked to him for a while, though he didn't respond, then the mother brought him back the next day and the next until he had visited every day for a week. The following week, the boy gestured that he wanted to go back again, and the mom told her son, "No, you've seen him enough." But the boy spoke his first words ever and said, "Take me to see the Standing Eagle." He'd never spoken before in his life—that was the first thing he said. The mom was so grateful she bought the car and had it delivered. He told her he didn't know how to drive and the car wasn't useful to him, but she said she wasn't picking it up; she didn't take back gifts, so now it just sat there. I told him I could teach him how to drive, and he offered to teach me about Native American medicine in exchange. I visited Standing Eagle a few times afterward. He did energy work on Lexi and sang songs of healing. She seemed to be healing up nicely. His energy work was very different from the way Marty had worked on me.

The restaurant that I worked at would get a variety of people. It was near the airport, and we would get many celebrities who would come to Houston and stop in for a drink or dinner. Our place was usually recommended by the hotels in the area. After meeting several celebrities, I began to notice there were differences in their energy fields.

The owner gathered us around and told us there was going to be a tarot card reader sitting in a booth every Wednesday, and whoever wanted a reading could walk over and get one. He felt like it would be good for business and add to the ambiance. *A tarot card reader?* I thought. I remembered that I had a deck of cards that I'd found in my grandma's house when she passed. The cards were from the 1940s, and they were called Old Gypsy. I didn't think she knew they were there; they probably belonged to one of my cousins. They came with a set of instructions along with definitions of what every card meant. I didn't really go through them—in fact, I never even pulled a card for myself. When my mom packed up some things from her house for me, she dropped in a couple of decks of tarot cards that were in a closet. I told her they weren't mine, and she said, "Oh, those must have been something your brother bought, and he doesn't want them." She pushed them away and said, "Just take them." I took the box home, and since it had a bunch of photos and whatnot, I slid the whole box into the back of my closet.

When I got to work on Wednesday, I was excited to see the tarot reader. What was the mystic being going to look like? She was bending over a table, covering it with a scarf that she must have brought from home. As she turned around, she was wearing a long flowing skirt, and she had the biggest set of boobs I'd ever seen. I was sure that was the attraction when the owner decided to bring her in on Wednesdays. Her energy field was red in a light way, and it had some swirls going on around the lower half of the body. I hadn't seen that before and thought I would go up and introduce myself. When I approached the table, she was looking over my shoulder at the people coming in the door. I asked her how long she'd been reading cards and why she started. She began shuffling the deck, and as she did, she said, "The renaissance festival." As she half-heartedly answered me, she explained she started reading at a festival and had been doing it ever since. She pulled a few crystals from her bag and set them on the table with a sign that read, "Tarot readings $10." The people who frequented the place would pay ten dollars for a rose when the rose lady came around, but I didn't feel the tarot reader would be there long since she wouldn't see the money she might expect. Besides, I felt she really knew nothing except what was on the instructions to the deck itself. As I walked to the waitress station, Paulette, a coworker, was squatting down, rifling through her purse, when she pulled out a ten-dollar bill. She stood, and with satisfaction in her energy field showing bright blue burst with gold, she headed over to the tarot table while mumbling, "Please watch my tables."

After thirty minutes with the tarot lady, she came back to the waitress station and picked up her tray. I said, "Wait a minute, tell me what she told you."

She set down the tray, and at that point, I noticed her field was sad. She said, "That woman is fake."

"Why do you say that?" I asked, already knowing from just standing in front of the woman.

Paulette explained how she told her that she needed to learn not to be picky with men, that she never got along with her mother, and that was the key to her life getting better. She said, "Nothing else she said applied to me either." Paulette was the best tester for the tarot reader since she had an unusual upbringing that only a person with genuine abilities would tap into. She was raised by an uncle who was amazing and took her in after her parents were killed in a crash. He was in the military. Paulette married the love of her life from junior high, and they had five kids. The generic reading she received was noticeably inaccurate.

Over the next few weeks, I watched the tarot reader's energy and the energy of the people who sat with her. I noticed nothing changed in her field as she read, and it didn't appear anything helpful was being shared with anyone. The tarot reader stopped showing up after she mentioned to one of the waitresses that it wasn't worth her time any longer. At that moment, I knew I'd seen what I needed to see and how I needed to see it, right down to Paulette's experience. The energy of the tarot reader never shifted, and that was a clear sign that she was not connecting to a field beyond the physical plane where spirits come in to communicate.

Chapter Five

The Glow

I was still having the recurring dream about primitive community bathrooms that had started in childhood around the time I'd visited the USS *Lexington*. I knew there was something to it because I would see more and more unfold before waking up. In the dream, I managed to guide myself to a shop so I could see my reflection, which showed me I was around seven years old. At that point, I knew it was a trauma I needed to clear from that life. A man began to appear in my dreams after I would see the restrooms. I would see him prior to waking up, usually feeling scared as if I had been running. My cat, Lexi, would usually come and sit on my chest as I was waking up.

A few years had passed, and I was twenty-six years old. The man I was dating, Richard, had started his own promotional management firm. We had been together for a while when we found out I was pregnant. A month after our daughter, Breezy, was born, he strongly urged me to marry him. His mother would say, "What would Breezy think if her parents weren't married?" I didn't feel Breezy would mind as long as she knew she was loved. However, the pressure was unbearable, and

I caved in. We went to the courthouse and got married. I never felt it was permanent and looked at it as a phase in my life.

I would say my prayers every night that God would lead me to what I was supposed to be doing. I wasn't working, so I spent my time volunteering. I spent extra time at a non-denominational church that had recently dropped "Baptist" from its name to be seen as more evolved.

I had begun working with Richard in building the management firm and securing promotion gigs. Richard was smart, perhaps smarter than he gave himself credit for. When we first got together, we didn't have much, yet I knew we would be millionaires before we were thirty. He laughed and said, "I don't know how that's going to happen, but if you think so, then we probably will."

Richard landed a big job for a major corporation, and when he received his first check, he was excited. It was the largest sum we had ever received in one check—sixty thousand dollars. He said, "If you think you're going to be a millionaire, then maybe we should look at investing in the market." I told him I didn't know anything about the stock market, but he insisted. He said, "Here are a few stocks I took a look at; perhaps you could look to see which ones stand out."

I glanced at the list, and my eyes took their own direction right to CMGI. "CMGI. That's the one I feel drawn to," I said. It was a penny stock, and we had nothing to lose since we felt we were young enough to make the 60K back if we lost it. He said, "Okay, then I'm going to invest sixty thousand in CMGI, and we'll see what happens." We had no idea how stock market accounts worked, but we invested the 60K in a Morgan Stanley Dean Witter account. Before we knew it, the account reached 2.2 million dollars. I didn't focus on the money we made since I felt 2.2 million dollars was not a lot, and we needed to stay focused on work.

HOW I FOUND MY SUPERPOWERS

***

We lived in a neighborhood that had an interesting array of people. My neighbor Joeleen, who had been worried about her health, came by the house letting me know the doctor had found a tumor in her abdomen and she needed to have surgery in the morning. She asked if I could take care of her kids the next day when they got home from school. That night when I got ready for bed, I kneeled down and began to pray for Joeleen. Typically, my prayers were right around forty-five minutes long, so when I was finished, I was extremely tired and had to go to bed. As I stood up from kneeling, I lay down and had a vision of Joeleen in the hospital bed talking to a doctor. I'd had visions like that before, but nothing so important, and nothing that I could share that would be well-received. Early the next morning, I went over to Joeleen's house, and she was getting ready to leave. I explained to her that sometimes I knew things or saw things, and they would happen. She seemed intrigued, so I told her I'd been shown that the tumor she had was benign. While the doctors had originally explained that there were usually three characteristics to that kind of tumor, it would only have two, and she wouldn't have any treatment after it was removed.

She looked at me in disbelief and said, "How do you know this?" I explained to her that the doctor would come and stand on the right side of her hospital bed. He would tell her he had good news—that the tumor was successfully removed and it only had two of the characteristics he had expected. She would then ask to see the tumor, but he would reply, "We cut it into pieces to be examined, and afterward, we discarded it."

Joeleen was in her head with worry and didn't believe what I was telling her. Later that evening, I got a call from a very awake Joeleen, and she said, "I don't know how you knew, but honest to God, Katharine, you were right. It was just like you said. The doctor stood on my right side, and word for word, he explained what you told me he would." Then she added, "Thank you for taking care of my kids. I'm going to get some sleep now."

During the remainder of the time I knew Joeleen, she would periodically be shocked at how I knew things. Often she would ask Richard, "How does she just know these things," then she'd follow it with her typical, "Honest to God, Katharine." She was seemingly exasperated with me—as if there had to be some magic trick I hadn't disclosed.

***

Aside from my experience with Joeleen, my days were seemingly normal. However, toward the end of the summer, I had the craziest experience one night while I was asleep. I was flying in the air as if it were nothing at all, and for some reason, I knew exactly where I was going. The air was circling me, and I was absolutely aerodynamic when all of a sudden, a spirit going the same speed stopped right in front of me. Our bodies straightened up from the flying position, and not speaking a word, our throat chakras opened, and there was a flow of light between us. I acknowledged him and expressed how much I'd missed him and wanted to be with him. He told me the same and began to send a frequency through the throat chakra. Then I felt a stronger emotion than the experience of making love on Earth. The frequency that we were sending back and forth to each other held such passion that it was a full-body orgasm. There's no human word I could come up with that could describe what happened that night. When the visit was over, we exchanged a love emotion, then flew back in opposite directions.

When I woke up, it was seven o'clock in the morning, and I was lying next to Richard. I knew it wasn't Richard who I'd been with in the night. The spirit figures we embodied in the dream were completely different in height and appearance from our physical bodies on Earth. Despite how familiar he was to me, I knew I hadn't met him in the physical plane yet during this lifetime. After such a powerful experience, the first thing I wanted to do was look for that person. Somehow I knew I would be crossing paths with him, and the experience would be incredible. The most fascinating thing about our encounter was that there was no body movement at all—it was all frequency. I felt some guilt for having had that experience while being married. I wasn't one to have sexual dreams, so it was completely out of the norm. I also knew it wasn't just a dream; that night, I knew it was something that actually happened on the spirit side, as I felt completely changed.

I continued to work, trying to put aside thoughts of the man with the frequency that gave me full-body orgasms.

Richard landed a great job opportunity traveling back and forth to London. He was working for a very established company that had locations in all the major cities. One day, I had just left church after getting everything ready for vacation Bible school. It was a week-long event, and I needed to put everything I had into getting the church decorated. My house was situated behind the building, with a large park that separated the neighborhood from the parking lot. I would walk to and from the building as needed. One day while I was walking home and holding my daughter's hand, I saw a vision of Richard rolling on a bed with a woman having sex. I quickly glanced up, knowing I could look around the room as if I were physically there. It was a hotel room with a small sign on the back of the door. I had the instant knowledge of it being London and that it was happening at that moment. While I was still in the hotel room, I heard my daughter's voice call "mommy" twice. I looked down, and we were still holding hands, walking toward home. I was then very aware of where I was. I was in London in that flash of a moment, then I was back in The Woodlands, and my physical body was in motion, crossing a soccer field.

I immediately went home and rested. My mind was playing through all the times I had seen something like that before. Perhaps I hadn't been aware in those times that I could have stepped into the space I was viewing while being somewhere else.

Richard called that night, and I handed the phone to Breezy. The next morning, I had a photo session set to get a promotional headshot for work. The photographer took a few extra pictures of Breezy and me together. Breezy insisted that Daddy would love a picture of his girls together. My comical side wanted to say, "Okay, but you will have to go to London to get the picture of Dad's other girl."

I couldn't shake the vision and the questions. *Why would he beg me to marry him and still do this?* After all, I had suggested we should get a divorce, but he hadn't agreed. *He is spineless*, I thought. He could have just said, "Let's get a divorce," and I would have happily obliged. A couple of years prior, Richard had worked with a major band and was involved in promotions for one of its members. A sexy Jewish rocker would call for Richard every night as soon as his concert ended and he'd returned to his tour bus or hotel room. When I would tell him Richard wasn't there, I knew he was enjoying our conversation and wanted to keep talking. I had to admit, I liked talking to him too, and he alluded to me jumping on the bus with him and leaving Richard a note. I was really mad I didn't get on that tour bus and go. I could see

Breezy adapting well to a new life on the road, as she'd already been to over three hundred concerts by that time in her life just being at work with me.

At that time, I felt I needed to go and talk to my pastor, Chris. He was very approachable, nonjudgmental, and respected. When I got to the church office, I stuck my head in while giving the door a knock. I asked if I could talk to him. He said, "Sure, Katharine, please have a seat. What's going on?"

I told him, "This may seem weird, but I often know and see things that other people don't know or see."

He held his hand up to stop me and said, "Close the door."

I got up, closed the door, and sat back down. "There are things I just know and visions that I have."

He said, "I feel guided to tell you that God is preparing you for more than you can imagine right now." He folded his hands together softly in front of him on his desk. "Many people at the church wouldn't agree with what I'm about to tell you, but God has given you the ability of vision so you would be able to help thousands of people."

Touched by his words, I explained my situation in my marriage—that I never wanted to marry Richard to begin with, and I had guilt over wanting a divorce.

He said, "Don't worry. You'll be guided as you wait for God to show you what's next on your journey." Pastor Chris knew how to give insightful counsel, and at that moment, I'd never appreciated him more.

When Richard came home that night, I didn't say a word. I thought I'd let him get settled first. Breezy had been trying to get the photo we recently took together into a photo frame. She finally mastered the job and was trying to slide it into Richard's computer bag. I was making dinner, and she said, "It won't fit."

I urged her to move his stuff over to make space for the frame. My patience with Richard was spent, and I could think of so many other places for that frame, none of which were appropriate for a child to hear.

Breezy pulled out an instant Polaroid of a woman smiling. She held it up and said, "Mommy, who's this?"

It's the woman who's been rolling around on the bed with Daddy, I secretly thought. I called Richard into the kitchen and asked Breezy to go to her room and play. She set the picture down on the kitchen island. When Richard came in, I held up the photo and asked, "Who's this?"

His energy field was red-orange, signaling fear and anger mixed. "Where did you get that?" He lunged forward in hopes of grabbing the picture.

With a smirk, I said, "I want a divorce. I know you've slept with her in a hotel room in London."

His mouth gaped open and his cheeks reddened before he grabbed his computer bag and scurried off to the bedroom. Over his shoulder, he yelled, "Are you having me followed?"

"No." I smiled. "Why have you followed when I could see you for myself with my own eyes?"

"You're freaking me out," he yelled before slamming the door.

***

While I was sitting out front in my yard, a passing neighbor told me she was sorry I was going through a divorce. She asked, "What are you going to do?"

I heard the frequency come in, and it said, "She knew he had a girlfriend."

I looked at her and asked, "Did you know all along?"

She nodded and told me he'd shared everything with her. "Why don't you just take yourself up to the country club and sit on the curb?" she asked. "Some guy would come along and pick you up."

"I'm not going down like that," I replied.

Richard left for London, and I filed for divorce. I soon learned there was nothing left in the investment account. I was starting over and completely broke.

I was working three jobs, trying to maintain the bills. I had two cars that we owned jointly that couldn't be sold until the divorce was finalized. Regina, my next-door neighbor, was a real busybody. She made everything her business. I worked from early morning until late night, and she would complain about my trash cans not being brought in after pickup. I told her, "I can't bring them in until nine or ten at night, and the HOA says I can bring them in the next morning anyway." But that wasn't good enough for her, and she began bringing my trash cans up and leaving them in front of my garage doors. That made it completely impossible for me to pull into the garage without having to get out of the car and move the cans. This continued for several weeks when I noticed a spot on the garage where she must have scraped it with the handle of the can because the paint was flaking off. I received a letter from the HOA asking me to repair the garage door where the paint was worn.

She even called the police on me several times a week, complaining about my dog barking. The dog lived inside with a doggy door to go out when needed. The police would come by and sneak up to the fence yet hear no barking. Amused, they would come to the door and explain that the neighbor next door was calling all the time about the trash cans and dog.

With every call, the sheriff's department would dispatch an officer, and I would get the most handsome guys in the department. My best friend would say, "How is it that you are the only one with a charming Adonis just showing up on your doorstep?"

I would tease her and say, "I have a rotten neighbor, and this is God's way of rewarding me."

I did end up dating one of the officers—okay, a couple of the officers. But I drew the line at that, as I didn't want to be known as a badge bunny. As far as the war that Regina started, I knew I had to do something. So Wednesday morning, before I left for work, I put the trash out like normal. There needed to be an extra treat for Regina when she grabbed the handle of my trash that night and dragged the bins to the garage door. I went into the backyard while wearing plastic gloves and picked up two large mounds of dog poop. I evenly smeared it, completely coating the handle of my garbage cans. The trash truck picked up the containers using a mechanical arm that came out from the side of the vehicle, so there was no worry about the poop being wiped off. I drove to work that morning singing the whole way as I imagined Regina's disgust when she had dog poop all over her hands. I couldn't stop laughing throughout the day; it actually made my day brighter. When I got home, only one of the cans had been pulled up the driveway; the other one was halfway up the driveway. I knew she probably began to smell the poop when she grabbed the second can.

That night when I prayed before bed, I felt God say, "Do not pray for her to move; pray that she is offered an amazing job and can afford a better place." I began to pray for that for the next week, and in a month, she told all the neighbors her husband had been offered a great job, and they were moving to Michigan. I smiled and thanked God, then said a quick prayer for the good people of Michigan.

***

As time went by, I met a guy named Forest, and we became a support system for each other, as we'd each gone through a divorce. We became very good friends, and neither of us was seeing anyone else.

After Breezy was born, I'd wanted another child but couldn't get pregnant. I had been to the doctor, and he told me everything was fine. When my divorce from Richard had been finalized, I'd resigned myself to the fact that I would only have one child and was grateful. During the time I was seeing Forest, there was a night that Breezy and I were watching *The Brady Bunch*, and I saw a vision of an IV in my left arm and a nurse handing me a baby on my left side. His hair was straight and long for a baby. I wondered why she hadn't handed the baby to me on my right side when my right arm was free from an IV. *Wait a minute*! I thought. *A baby boy? Oh, wow—am I pregnant?* I knew the soul was coming and had a special purpose, as all souls do, and I was eager to find out what that purpose was.

I took a pregnancy test the next day, and I was pregnant. When I told Forest, we both agreed he would relinquish all parental rights so he would have no financial support obligation. We were very close, but we wanted different things in life. I wanted the child, and he never saw himself becoming a dad. I saw it as the perfect agreement so we could go our separate ways.

It was summertime when I was pregnant with Zach. The neighborhood I lived in was still selling new homes, and my friend Summer worked for the home builder. She worked six days a week and was exhausted. Since I lived so close, she asked if I would be interested in helping by sitting in the office located in the dining room of one of the show homes at the front of the neighborhood. I was excited to be doing something different and making some extra cash. The hours were short since she only needed me to relieve her for lunch. She showed me a stack of the builder's design options and floorplans that needed to be placed in folders. I began filling the folders and decided to finish all of them as a surprise for Summer. As I was making my way through the stack, a couple walked in. The guy seemed happy to be there, but the woman seemed nervous. I offered to show them around, but he said, "There's no need for that; I just wanted to show her a few things upstairs." So I waved them on and was grateful they didn't need any attention while I continued to work through the folders. Fifteen minutes later, they came back downstairs. I was so focused on my task that I had forgotten they were even there. They said thank you and left.

The door swung open one minute later, and Summer popped in. She asked, "Did that couple go upstairs?"

I said, "Yes, he told me he wanted to show her something."

Summer turned red and hurried up the stairs, saying something like, "The builder is on his way here now." As she rushed to get upstairs, I couldn't make out what else she said, so I hurried behind her with curiosity. We landed in the bedroom that had a beautiful view of the front drive. The bedspread was in disarray, and the room had a stench. She explained that the couple would frequent new home models in the area and find a room they could revisit to have sex. He was a married businessman in the area, and they were coworkers. She went on to explain that he liked that room because of the view of the front. He could see if someone walked or drove up.

She began to fix the bed, and I noticed a glow on the floor. She said, "This guy is gross. He flings his used condoms in the dresser drawer next to the bed or throws them onto the floor next to the wall."

I was intrigued by the glow on the carpet and asked, "What is that glowing area?" I reached down to the carpet to point it out.

"Don't touch it, for Christ's sake," Summer said, completely grossed out. After we straightened the room and checked the rest of the house, I was still thinking of the glow. Summer went out to her car to bring in a tray of sandwiches and cookies for the meeting with the builder. It had been twelve minutes since we were upstairs, so I journeyed back to see the carpet. The glowing substance had almost completely faded away. It had a similar glow to that around a living object.

I lived only a block away, and as I walked home, I thought about how the glow died off. It must have been semen on the carpet that produced the glow. I decided to bank that information and not discuss it with anyone. Explaining it to Summer or anyone else might make them see me as crazy.

Later that week, I had an Ob/Gyn appointment I was excited about. There was a woman sitting next to me in the office who was very excited too. She told me her pregnancy story of how she selected her sperm donor and the process she had to go through. While she was explaining her experience, my thoughts drifted. *How long does sperm live on the tile*? I wondered. The glow apparently wore off at the ten- to twelve-minute mark with fabric such as carpet. *Does that mean the sperm is inactive?* As I considered what I had seen, I thought to myself, *I could have sat next to anyone, and yet the universe found it to be important for me to hear this message*. I knew it was connected to what I had noticed with the glow on the model home floor. There was so much science behind those vials of sperm the woman described. I could imagine carpet being a real killjoy for the little guys.

I truly believe that when the universe wants to teach you something, if you aren't grasping or giving enough time to explore the learning opportunity, the universe will continue to bring it back and make you revisit the lesson.

***

As I was checking voicemails, there was one left from Ryan Schwartz, my teenage love. He said, "Hi, um, I don't know what to say. But I ran into your brother, and he told me you had been married and are divorced. Would you like to come to my daughter's birthday party this weekend?"

I thought that was sweet, and I was interested in seeing him and his daughter. When I arrived at the venue, it was a circus-themed party. So many kids were darting through the crowd of parents—then I saw Ryan. He was holding a balloon and smiled big when he noticed me. Breezy and I walked toward him, and as he moved forward to give me a hug, I noticed his mom, Lily, sitting at the table behind him. Lily smiled big, and he noticed that she recognized me. When Breezy and I approached the table, Lily reached for my hand, and with tears filling her eyes, she explained how sorry she was for breaking Ryan and me up. I told her that everything worked out like it was supposed to. Later, Ryan explained that his mother had been struggling with guilt about that for the past five years, and she was truly sorry. At the end of the party, I thanked them for inviting me and hugged them both. I knew when I saw Lily she would be crossing to the other side soon, and the situation she put Ryan and me through was something she needed to clear from her conscience. After the birthday party, I didn't meet up with Ryan again. I knew I'd gone to the party for peace and closure.

***

The Texas heat was more than I could stand walking home from my part-time house-sitting job. As I approached my street, my neighbor Tracy, who lived a few houses down, waved and gestured for me to come over. I was one of only two neighbors who were nice to her. The other neighbor ladies thought she and her husband Brett were snobby and only invited her to the Pampered Chef parties they would host. I really didn't feel like visiting with her since I knew Breezy's school bus would be pulling up soon. I tried waving her off, but she walked down and insisted I come inside her house to look at the armoire she wanted to list for sale so I could give my opinion on what I thought a fair price would be.

"You're home early," I said, remembering that Tracy never beat the school bus home. Tracy turned around beaming and told me that her best friend from college, Margo, had been offered a job at a huge firm in Houston and was staying with them until she found a place. As we approached the house and I was admiring her snapdragons that were in full bloom, she told me Brett was mad at her for agreeing to let Margo stay with them. Tracy leaned in, partially covering her mouth, and whispered, "I thought Brett would be mad because he never wanted to hang out with her when we were in college."

She opened the front door. I immediately saw Margo, who was looking a little flush. Brett was focused on what appeared to be a soccer game. My eyes directed me to the cushion next to Brett. *Hey, wait a minute*, I thought, *there's that glow again—the same one on the rug.*

I felt nervous, and I didn't know why. Perhaps I was feeling bad for Tracy. Since Summer couldn't see the glow on the carpet, I knew she couldn't see the glow on the cushion. Margo stood up and stepped forward to shake my hand. At the same moment, I stepped behind Tracy and reached for the door handle while announcing that I had to go. I stepped outside, thankful to have escaped shaking her hand since I was positive she had a role in the glow on the cushion.

***

After Zach was born, life seemed to go smoothly. He and Breezy were busy with normal activities that kept me busy too. Things continued that way for a few years. I was feeling an occasional panic attack, but it was nothing I couldn't shake off at first. They would come out of nowhere with no real triggers at all. As time went on, that made them increasingly difficult to manage. It got so bad I couldn't even get in the car and drive to the corner of the street. My friends were concerned since I had been driving into Houston or Galveston several times a week, and now I couldn't even visit with them. I eventually asked Carmen, a mom from my son's class, to start picking him up for preschool in the mornings. Carmen asked, "What's going on?"

I explained that the anxiety attacks had been so bad I couldn't even be around people.

She said, "There's an amazing woman who helped me after I returned home from Desert Storm. She does energy work and a couple of other things. You should give her a call. Her name is Belinda Smart—let me give you her phone number."

On the day of the appointment, I wasn't quite sure what to expect. I was told to call Belinda at 12:15. Carmen warned me not to be a minute late, or I'd have to reschedule. When I called, I explained what I'd been going through with the anxiety and how I was to the point that anytime I went around anybody, their energy fields made me want to run home.

"Okay," she said. "Let me take a look at you. Can you lie down?"

I lay on the bed and put the phone on speaker.

The first thing she said was, "Wow, you are rather thin." At the time, I was somewhere around a hundred pounds. "You're coming into your own spiritual awakening, and it's time for you to walk rather than avoid it."

I told her about the things that would happen to me when I was younger, the things that I knew. She said, "You pushed it down so you wouldn't get in any trouble. You were meant to walk the path of a healer. The first thing you're going to do is get your power back." Belinda began the session, and toward the end, I felt much better. I asked if I would need to do sessions like the ones she offered. Belinda explained everyone has their own way of communicating with their spirit guides. Everyone has different gifts, and when she started her path, she only knew a few things, and one was how to ground. She allowed the universe to guide her, and I needed to be open to doing the same.

The following week, the session with Belinda went a little different outside the energy work. She asked me what I was doing for a job. I explained I hadn't been able to work. I had such anxiety that it kept me from leaving the house. Previously, I'd been writing restaurant reviews to all the restaurants I'd been visiting, which was one every single day up until the anxiety took over. She said, "The first thing you're going to do is to get a job outside the house again. What's around your place?"

I mentioned the giant grocery store right outside of my neighborhood. She said it was a great place to go and get a job.

"Okay, maybe that will be good. I've always thought it would be fun to work in a bakery. Maybe the store would hire me for the bakery."

She said, "That's perfect."

When I went into the grocery store, I carefully assessed the quickest exit in the event I needed to leave from a panic attack. When I made it to the customer service counter, I was gripping it to continue to remind myself, *I am here, and I am safe*. I filled out an application, and the girl behind the counter, whose name tag read "Rosie," said the manager would like to talk to me that day. She told me to go and sit in the lobby of the coffee shop.

I was really nervous as I sat, waiting for the manager. When she finally got there and sat down, I tried not to focus on any feelings I was picking up from her. What could I focus on? I looked at what she was wearing and noticed a small round sticker. *Ah, now that's nice*, I thought. I read "I donated today" and saw the illustration of a drop of blood. *Oh no, not donating blood. Blood makes me squeamish; that's why I never went into the medical field.* I glanced at her earrings and noticed they were almost the same color as her energy field. *Oh no, not the energy field. You have to focus on something else.* The necklace was beautiful—I recognized it as a signature piece that perhaps came with a robin-egg-blue bag. *What am I doing?* I realized I'd missed everything she said while fighting through the avoidance of a full panic. When I zoned back in to what she was actually doing, I saw her marking the back of the application with the words, "Barista. Location: coffee shop." She said, "I'll let the coffee shop manager know that you'll be their new addition."

What did I miss? I thought. *Now I'm a barista. I don't even know how to make coffee.*

The next morning, I showed up for work. There were two other employees working the shift. One was Athena, a beautiful Greek goddess, and the other was a young guy crouching down behind the coffee machine doing espresso shots. I was not one for the register, but I loved making the drinks. When people would come up and order, I would watch their energy. A few times, I would look at them and say, "I know what you want," then I would proceed to tell them what they were about to order. I turned it into a complete carny. It was fun to see their reaction as they would exclaim, "Yes! How did you know?"

Of course we had our regulars, and they were my study. I noticed a shift in their energy fields before and after their morning coffee. The coffee seemed to numb their senses the same way alcohol does. A weird film would come over their field after consumption.

Everyone working at the coffee shop had an interesting story, and everyone who worked there had a college degree. I was the only one who just had a high school diploma. My anxiety wasn't gone, I was still struggling with it, but I focused on the space behind the counter as my home base and thought of myself as being protected. I liked to stay behind the coffee machine since there I felt like I had a good distance between me and anyone who would come up to the counter. But there were a few times when I had to step up and take an order when a coworker slipped away to go to the bathroom.

The avoidance of noticing the customers' energy was difficult, and one morning it was really hard. A lady walked up to the counter to order a drink. She glanced down at a stack of catalogs that Athena brought in to look through during our break. She asked, "Are those your catalogs?"

"Yes, Athena brought them in for us to look through," I replied.

On top of the stack was a Ralph Lauren catalog, and the woman said, "I didn't think you two could afford Ralph Lauren on what you make." Her face scrunched up while strolling to the end of the bar to pick up her drink.

I glanced at her energy field. It had shields running up and down; there was a man in her field, which indicated that she was married, but I also sensed that they were not in love. I immediately felt sad for her. The frequency came in again and said, "This is usually the source for why humanity lashes out at one another; being unfulfilled has led to generations of people not accepting themselves." *Not accepting themselves? What does that mean?* The frequency came across again and simply said, "Self-love."

Later that afternoon, I had an appointment with Belinda. It had been several weeks since I'd last spoken to her. She asked about the job. "It's great; I'm a barista now!" I explained. "I don't know anything about coffee; in fact, I can't even stand it, yet I'm having so much fun."

She was happy for me and suggested that we see what my guides had been working on lately as she reminded me to feel my feet rooting into the earth. That was an important element of grounding.

Toward the end of the session, she said, "You're getting your power back after years of pushing down trauma that is finally ready to clear." I knew meeting Belinda was exactly what I needed along my path and was grateful.

The local community college was teaching Reiki and herbal healing, so I decided to take the classes. I began doing energy work and practicing with friends. I loved the fact I could work on myself whenever I needed to. Thinking back to what I had learned from Standing Eagle on herbs, it was all beginning to make sense—everything seemed to be flowing right. I was still having difficulty driving very far, but at least I was out driving.

Chapter Six

The Leaving

While I was out running errands one day, I felt guided to stop at a resale shop. There was only one other woman shopping. I could feel her energy, and immediately, she was right next to me. She asked if I had visited the gifts and herbs shop up the road. Since I was not in a conversation with her and was minding my own business, I thought, *That's a strange thing for her to ask*. After I left the resale shop, I had a little bit of time, so I decided to go check out the herb shop.

When I walked in, the woman behind the counter who wore a name tag that read "C.J." looked at me and said, "Well, what took you so long?" She had a big smile on her face and was beaming with light as if she'd been waiting for me. C.J. was about the same age as my mother. She walked me around the store, showing me unique items. As I was looking, I noticed from the corner of my eye that she kept staring at me like she was waiting for me to recognize her. I felt uncomfortable but not uncomfortable enough to leave. After all, I wasn't being held against my will. We talked for a few hours before I realized the time, and I had to leave and go pick up Zach. She was clearly sad that I had to go and insisted I come back to continue our conversation.

The next morning, I woke up thinking about C.J., so the first thing I had to do was go to see her. She began the conversation by telling me things about my upbringing no one else would have known. C.J. knew I saw auras and markings in the energy field. She also knew I could see into the body. But what I felt the most drawn in by was when she told me she was supposed to be my mother. I'd never told anyone about the things my mother said and how she never wanted me. I would fantasize about having a mom who really wanted me, which was something I didn't talk about.

She asked if I would be interested in working there and offered to pay me with products she sold in the store and to teach me about my gifts. I told her I didn't know anything about vitamins or herbs. She explained that she'd been a nurse for forty years and was very strong with intuition, giving her the ability to look into the human body. "By focusing on the energy field, we know what the body needs." She told me she had several doctors who would send patients over to her shop for her to look into their bodies.

At that moment, two women walked in, and one of the ladies said, "Dr. Lewinski sent me over to see C.J."

C.J. turned to me and said, "Take a look at her energy field."

I looked, and she asked me what I saw. I described what I was being shown. C.J. turned to the woman and explained what I was referring to, outlining in detail what was going on with her body. C.J. then went to the counter and filled out a piece of paper for her to take back to the doctor, keeping a copy for herself. The two ladies left, and C.J. told me that I belonged with her—she was the only one who could show me what I needed to learn and how I was to help others. I began working there the next day. I spent every day with her that I could, not just so she could teach, but because, for the first time, I had a mother figure who wanted me. I was still working at the coffee shop for a paycheck, so I balanced my time.

After a few weeks of working for C.J., she announced that she planned to go back to teaching psychic development classes. She asked if I would help. *How would I help her with the classes?* I thought. *I'm still developing my own gifts and have a lot to learn.* The following week, C.J. had scheduled the first Wednesday night class. Word had begun to spread quickly. On the first night, there were fifteen people, and every week after that, it continued to grow. Some nights were much busier than others, and the class often brought in people who weren't of the light. It was easy for me to discern. Their energy was very dark and usually marred with anger, hate, pornography, and other negative and noxious markers.

As C.J. began to open to channel a message, I felt an energy come into my throat that freaked me out. I kept trying to clear my throat and swallow. C.J. noticed that the archangel she was asking to channel was trying to come into me to speak. It was a very strange feeling that frightened me. When I asked C.J. about the feeling, she said I was an open channel and the ascended master wanted to communicate with the group.

I was super delighted to be working alongside her. It was nirvana having that maternal energy of acceptance that I desperately craved. The crazy thing was many people who met us would think she was my mother.

My own mother was MIA. Any bridge we had begun to build with the birth of Breezy and Zach was destroyed around that time when we suddenly became homeless. Mom didn't even offer us shelter, even though she knew we would be sleeping in our car. She told me, "You will figure something out; you always do."

When the Wednesday classes started, I greeted the attendees at the door. It seemed that everybody was super excited to be there, and most everyone was a hugger. I would only hug a few people. When someone came in, I saw their energy and would determine if I wanted to be embraced by what was happening in their field. Those who had dark energy were the ones I didn't interact with, as I knew they weren't truly ready to change. Their choice to embrace things such as porn, drugs, and judgments kept them from standing in the light of God.

Even handshakes are a sly way to get information from others—a handshake is an instant download of knowledge. Those not completely spiritually awakened would be able to shake hands to get a good read on another individual, and since I knew some of those attending had dark energy in their fields, I avoided physical contact with them. The right hand is the receiver, and the left is the giver, similar to a battery. When we shake someone's right hand, that unawakened individual can download knowledge on us. Because of that, I never shook hands with anyone, and when someone extended their hand, I would say, "I don't shake hands."

In spiritual classes, there were always more females than males. It was a seven to three ratio. The males who showed up were always given great attention since they were rare—some of the ladies in the class actually had a hard time focusing on anything but them. I think it had to do with the fact that they were interested in the same thing, and that made the guys super sexy. It was kind of funny since, by appearance, most would probably not be found sexy in any other group. I wasn't so easily swayed by the guys who attended. One fun and interesting part of being in the class was when I would hear the thoughts of someone next to me, and they were thinking about one of the guys.

There was one in particular who everyone seemed to like. His name was James. James was a local commercial builder, and he was also a recovering alcoholic. He really got into meditating after rehab in hopes of clearing his energy field and life of anything that was toxic or negative. He had begun to drop by the store more regularly since I'd started working, often visiting between jobs. I overheard him inquiring about me to C.J. one day. He asked her what I could see. I was flattered to think he would ask about me since he looked like he didn't have trouble meeting women. He was the kind of guy women of all ages threw themselves at shamelessly.

One night during class, he sat toward the front, and I could hear his thoughts about my feet. *Feet?* I thought. I couldn't hold back a smirk and thought, *I'm about to torture this guy.* I kicked off my shoes and stretched my feet out. My feet were freshly manicured from the weekend and, of course, topped off with the most neon orange I could find. The color could stop traffic at night. I could tell by his thoughts he was super excited. Sadly, I knew he was also unable to focus. While my eyes were still on C.J., I thought perhaps I should stop the shenanigans. I tuned into what C.J. was talking about and could hear her mental note: *Talk to me tomorrow about using gifts the wrong way.*

The next morning I was nervous about the thought of C.J.'s disapproval of my behavior. What was the harm? After all, nobody in the class would ever know what I was doing, and of course, James had no idea that I knew what he was thinking. When I arrived, James's truck was there. As I approached the door, James opened it wearing a big grin and his favorite shirt. It was green with Buddha on the front. He never said it was his favorite shirt, but he wore it often—I knew it to be his favorite. When I saw him, he was glowing. His energy field was yellow, which meant pure happiness. In his hand, there was a Big Gulp cup, and he had a few of his crew members close behind him. They chatted for a bit and left.

C.J. turned to me and said, "I'm going to teach you about free will." I thought to myself, *Free will Thursday.* She explained that while she was in college, she had no idea that when she thought of a guy, they thought of her. She explained that any time she sent a mental message, they would show interest in her and not know why. I thought about all the times that I had done similar things. The sheepish grin on my face vanished, and I began to understand that there was truth in her teaching. As connected as I was feeling to the spiritual realm, I suddenly felt the distance, too, all in one blow. She told me she knew that I did the same thing with men. C.J. explained, "This is conjuring, and you don't want that. It will mess with your life."

While I had a few minutes with C.J., I told her I'd met a man in a dream several years before and that we were flying to see each other. She looked deep into my energy field and said, "This is the person you incarnated to be with. He was born a year before you. You've been visiting with him on the spirit side." I told her I hadn't had a dream about him since. She told me, "It wasn't important for you to continue to have dreams about him. You need to stay focused on your spiritual path. When you're meant to meet him, you will meet him, and nothing will stand in your way." I knew she was right, as what I truly wanted was to find out why I had those abilities and what I was to do with them.

After lunch, a young woman came in, hoping to have C.J. look at her body and see what was going on with her cycle. C.J. took a deep look into the woman, then turned to me and asked me to scan her.

Me? I thought. *Well, okay, let's go.* As I looked into her body, I noticed her fallopian tubes. There was a clamp on both of them, and one of the clamps had shifted. I noticed how they had been put in the same position, but one of them had moved out of place, showing where the fallopian tube was raw. As I explained what I was looking at,

I was shown an MRI machine that she was exposed to while with her son. The magnet from the MRI had moved the clamp. C.J. looked at her and asked, "Does this make sense?" The woman explained that her son fell during his baseball practice and needed to get an MRI. She was with him in the room while he was having it done. The woman was relieved to know it was nothing major and left to go see her doctor.

C.J. turned to me and said, "I want you to take an anatomy class. That way, you'll know exactly what you're looking at when you peer into the body."

Anatomy? I thought. *Is all that really necessary?*

She added, "I also want you to take iridology." I asked why. She said, "That area isn't as open to psychics, so it would be so much easier for you to be an iridologist here at the store. Iridology is the intricate study of eye tissue. All you have to do is take anatomy and learn the parts of the body. When people come in for iridology, you could photograph their eyes and write down everything you see within their body from the psychic perception level. The customers are going to think we have the best iridologist they have found anywhere."

I checked into the class and noticed they had one starting in the next couple of weeks. I was able to get both courses lined up in a reasonable timeframe to each other. In the weeks leading up to the classes, I noticed that as more people came into the store for C.J. to scan them, she would turn to me and ask what I saw. She told me she wanted me to really look at everything and that she was trying to train me.

C.J. was a Reiki master and would offer Reiki energy healing sessions in the back room. On my birthday, C.J. offered me a session. She said, "Rather than doing energy work, I would like to go through your childhood trauma and try to clear it." She had me sit in a chair, and she stood behind me. She carefully put her hands on the back of my head. We started off with a few things that happened when I was a baby. I hadn't told C.J. anything about my childhood other than how Mom didn't understand me. We went through each incident so I didn't have to say too many words. Every time she would pull up a trauma, I would witness it but without the pain. She got to one in particular, and I could see her pause. She said, "Look who's coming forward at this moment."

I saw Mother Mary walk forward. I was in a diaper playing in my room. Mom was standing at the door and laughing as she watched me pick up a piece of poop that fell out of my diaper and allowed me to try to eat it. As C.J. and I watched together, she verbally described the scene as Mother Mary came to take the child—me at a toddler age—to the light, offering her something good to eat. Mother Mary picked the child up and walked into the light with her.

C.J. continued with the regression, skipping some of the small stuff, trying to clear through the big stuff. We had been in the backroom for three hours, only getting to age nine. I told her I was tired, and I knew she was too. I hugged, kissed, and thanked her for loving me. We walked out to the parking lot together, and I felt free.

***

C.J. taught Reiki at one of the local community centers nearby. Each time I practiced with the Reiki energy, I could feel it as a soft tide coming into my field. While I'd waited those few weeks before starting the anatomy class, I took C.J.'s Reiki II class so I could progress in my learning. I felt so happy as I bounced into work every day with a pep in my step, and everything was going great. I had a mother figure who approved of and wanted me. The anatomy class seemed to come very easy. I didn't remember school feeling that effortless. It felt as though something had changed, but what? As I sat there thinking, I felt a frequency message say, "You're opening to connect."

What am I connecting to? I wondered.

The frequency came again and said, "God source."

At work one afternoon, I walked through the book section and noticed a new title called *How to Uncover Your Past Lives* by Ted Andrews. As I read the name Ted Andrews, I was told by the frequency that he'd recently passed into the light. There was a female next to me looking through the books. I introduced myself and asked her if I could help her with anything. She told me she was a yoga teacher and gave me her business card. It read, "Renee Dipsy, yoga teacher & massage therapist." She invited me to attend her class. Her next session was on the weekend, so I dropped in and brought my friend Maxine. Maxine was a butch lesbian and so good-looking that most women were attracted to her in some way. I knew Renee wasn't a lesbian and had never been with a female—that was easily attainable information from her energy field—but she shamelessly flirted with Maxine. She looked at her and said, "You know what I'm thinking." Then she turned to me and explained that when people are spiritually evolved, they can communicate by telepathy. However, I watched their energy fields, and there was nothing like that happening. Renee invited us back and insisted that she get Maxine's number.

On our way to lunch afterward, Maxine kept laughing about the whole telepathy thing. She said, "That's the first time I've ever had someone use telepathy to flirt." Such experiences had been teaching me an important new lesson. I'd grown confident in my ability to read a person's energy when they tried to send mental messages, and it had become very clear to me when the receptor of the other person was shut. When two people were communicating verbally, I'd also started to notice if one of them was closed off. I had learned that tuning in to recognize whether someone listened to another person helped me discern whether they really cared.

***

The week or two leading up to my decision to leave my job with C.J. seemed to be filled with one sign after another from the universe. How else could I leave that woman who made me feel accepted? The first red flag I noticed was in her energy field. It was a dark orange, and the edges were frayed. She normally carried a royal purple color in her field. When I thought about it, I realized there was a gradual change that had been taking place. The energy at the herb shop felt different too. One day, as I tried to push aside what I was noticing to get on with the daily chores of the shop, a lady walked in. She was dressed sharp and asked to see Claudette Johnson.

"C.J. is with a client. Would you like to have a seat?" I asked, offering her a nearby chair. "She will be out in fifteen min—"

Before I could finish my sentence, she walked straight into C.J.'s office. I heard the door fly open, and the client who was with C.J. bolted for the front door while glancing back in fear. The impatient lady came back out with satisfaction in her energy field. She turned her head while still moving toward the door and gave me a smile that showed no teeth as she left. Still looking through the glass from my post behind the counter, I turned my eyes away from the lady's car as it left the parking lot so I could focus on the counter where I was working. C.J. was suddenly standing in front of me. She was pale and had no color left in her field, only a smog-like appearance around her head and chest. I placed my hand on her shoulder; it was all I felt I could do, which felt odd because there had never been physical boundaries between us since day one.

As C.J. stared blankly into my eyes, she asked, "What did that woman's energy field show?"

I didn't miss a beat to answer as I said, "She was satisfied and accomplished." *Why is she asking me? Why can't she see for herself?* I thought.

At that moment, I heard the frequency again. "She has been blanketed with fear." *Blanketed?* I thought that was an interesting term to use.

C.J. informed me that the woman was with the IRS, and her husband, who handled the taxes, had not filed in four years. She began counting the register while telling me she needed to go see her husband. I said, "Sure," as I picked up my purse.

When I got home, I meditated, asking God what to do. I fell asleep while meditating, and a few hours later, I woke up to soft nudges from my seven-year-old informing me not to worry about making dinner since his uncle had taken him to McDonald's after school. *McDonald's?* I thought as I looked into his beautiful eyes, his one green and one brown eye looking back at me. He had a vivid yellow light in his field, which signified happiness, as he knew McDonald's was not on our approved list. However, I understood one meal was not my biggest concern at the moment.

The next morning on the way to work, I couldn't shake the feeling that I should tell C.J. I needed to find my own way. The parking lot was sparse. As I closed the car door, I noticed a woman leaving the shop with a beautiful energy field full of rainbow colors. I knew I couldn't get to the door fast enough to give a casual hello without seeming weird. When I walked into the shop, C.J. was pricing new products. My eyes took their own direction as I noticed a short stack of flyers on the counter with some business cards. The face of the woman who'd just left was printed on them. I asked C.J. about her while reaching to pick one up. She quickly slammed her hand down over the stacks and said, "She teaches energy work, and I just don't know if she's of the light," as she scooted them off the side of the counter and into the trash. C.J. pushed some vitamin bottles toward me and asked me to put them on the shelves. "Janice is coming in for a session," she announced, then casually added, "What do you get when I say her name?" That was typical C.J. training, so I didn't think anything about the question. As soon as I heard her say Janice's name, I followed the frequency of her image from C.J.'s thoughts to tap in for the reading. I noticed Janice coming into a grieving period with her mother—it appeared that her mom would be leaving this life soon due to pancreatic cancer. Then I saw she was having struggles in her marriage from loss of intimacy. I noticed her husband's energy because I was tuned into hers. I sensed that he had gone to the doctor for his blood pressure and was on medication to keep it in check. Janice was unaware of her husband going to the doctor, as he didn't want his diet monitored. That seemed to be the issue causing the lack of sex drive.

After telling C.J. what I was seeing, she was pleased, as she had guided me to look at everything I saw. This pattern had become so frequent that anytime anyone came into the shop or came into the class, she would ask me what I saw.

When Janice came in that day, C.J. was already in her office, so I directed her where to go. Once Janice was out of sight and I heard the door close, I reached down into the trash and picked out a flyer. It indeed belonged to the rainbow lady I had seen leaving the shop as I came into work. I folded up the flyer and put it inside my front pocket.

During C.J. and Janice's meeting, the store had become steady with customers and visitors who just wanted to come in and say hi. C.J. and

Janice emerged from the office. There were a few people who wanted to chat with C.J., so they stopped her in the back of the store. C.J. was in an extremely good mood, and her laughter was genuine. Janice grabbed a few items and then checked out. I heard a spirit say, "Ask her about her session," so as I was checking her out, I said, "How was your session with C.J.?"

Her smile was gentle as she said, "It was so informative! She told me several things that I knew about my mother, and there were a few things she told me that I didn't know about my husband. I believe them because I felt he was having issues, so I plan to talk to him."

As she left, I felt God's frequency again, and that time it said, "C.J. is blanketed. She told Janice everything you said as if it were her reading."

I was in a daze watching Janice leave and thought, *Blanketed—there's that word again.* The next few days, I was in class, so the only other employee, Rose, was filling in for me. I stopped by when I got out of class, and I could tell that Rose and C.J. had recently been talking about me. I could also tell that Rose had received a warning about me because she had pulled back her energy field. Rose was not tuned in to being psychic at all. She was laden with self-inflicted guilt and shame that she reminded herself of daily. She was a much older, kind woman who lost her son to a drug overdose when he was in his teenage years. He was her only child. At that point, he had been gone for fifty years. I would see her son's spirit come in when she mentioned him, and then he would leave afterward.

While I talked with Rose that day, C.J. left to make a trip to the bank. I had hoped chatting with Rose would give me a chance to read her energy so I could receive a message as to why she had become fearful of me. I knew Rose would not be able to hold back what her fear toward me was. As she showed me the new Himalayan salt lamps,

I asked how she was doing, and as she took her guard down to answer me, I tuned in to her field. I could tell that the mothering side of her, which she often displayed when given the chance, was itching to teach me something. She arranged the lamps while explaining, "Sometimes when people begin to tune in to the psychic world, they can go the wrong direction." She looked at me with pity, then went on to say that I was spending too much time in the spirit world. She told me that C.J. was worried about me and thought I was lost.

What! Seriously? I thought. *Why would C.J. say that?* God's frequency came in and said, "She is worried about losing her customers to you." I realized I might have stood there looking at Rose in silence for too long before responding. I could feel the spirit guiding me to take the high road and not lean into the ego of being upset. While looking her directly in her eyes, I simply responded by saying, "Everyone walking on Earth should be able to feel out their truth without being guided by the fears of others."

When I got home, I pulled out the flyer that I'd lifted from the trash. The name read, "Julie Snow." When I looked at her photo on the flyer and thought about her rainbow energy, I knew she would be the next step on my spiritual journey.

I grabbed the phone and dialed her number. She answered on the third ring. I introduced myself and told her I'd found one of her flyers and was interested in getting some energy work. She said, "I'll be in your end of town for a crystal bowl meditation Monday and will come by your place by two p.m." It felt good to make the appointment, given it was Thursday and the weekend would be soon, so I would have some time to think about how to tell C.J. I needed to leave the shop.

I began my prayer that night as usual, and I focused on connecting to God's source energy rather than just being open. I was feeling betrayed by C.J. and the words she had spoken against me. When my eyes couldn't shed another tear and I was feeling low, I collapsed into bed and gazed at the large amethyst geode on the dresser directly in front of me. I closed my eyes as they were getting heavy, then was nudged to reopen them. I saw a beautiful iridescent blue oval that was five feet by four feet. I opened and closed my eyes several times with great anticipation. Mother Mary was there in front of where the portal had been, and my focus shifted to her. My eyes began to tear up again, and I got out the words, "Have you come for me?"

She transmitted to me in a frequency with audio unlike I'd heard before. It sounded like I had a headset on. The amount of love and devotion I felt all at once was a rush. I immediately said, "I have many questions," and I got to my knees while still in bed. I held up my notes with questions that I'd been keeping since I began learning about communicating with the other side. I told her, "I've read the Bible many times, and great portions don't feel right. It doesn't seem to resonate with the source love I've been in touch with through the frequency." I knew God was the frequency. It was lucid—as if it could engulf me all at once in light and love. I showed her the Bible that I'd been reading. It was the Oxford NIV Study Bible. On the worn pages, I had highlighted the parts that were true and left unmarked parts that were not true.

She reminded me of an incident that had happened within my friend group in high school. She said, "Do you remember that you witnessed what happened, yet by the time the story got back around to you, it was completely different than what had really happened?"

"Yes," I shouted with excitement, "I remember that story exactly." I laughed in agreement that the rumor was completely different from the way it started.

She said, "That's right, and you are certain because you were there to witness exactly what happened." As I nodded, understanding her point, Mary shared with me, "While the Bible has many great stories, there are many great stories left out. There are parts that are explained by understanding what people believed to be God." She went on to clarify that most of the Old Testament was written about what the people of the time deemed God to be, which were actually extraterrestrials from other places who had special gifts. The New Testament, in contrast, encompassed much of the true source God, who is the creator of all.

When people of Old Testament times would encounter beings from other places who had special power, they began to worship and call those beings God. The men who told most of the Old Testament stories did not lie; they were sharing the stories that had been shared with them and the viewpoint of the people about the great beings of power they called Gods. I understood how it would be confusing for those who came across a being who could do extraordinary things, unlike what they had seen before.

I expressed to Mother Mary that several events stood out as not resonating with source love. The one that troubled me was Genesis 22, where it was written that God tested Abraham and told him to take his only son, Isaac, and sacrifice him. She placed her hand up and said, "Everyone needs to stop and feel with their hearts the truth. The being asking this of Abraham was an entity being worshiped as a God, not *the* God."

I said, "Okay, could you please explain Adam and Eve, Jesus dying for sins, and the truth behind why nations and languages were separated off in regions of the world?"

She began to explain to me that people were brought there in groups of various colors and various languages. It was never meant for any group to be against another group. That division was seeded from the greed man built through deviating from the source. She said,

"There will come a time in the next twenty years when those who still see us will be exiting Earth and have the opportunity to cycle again and elevate their soul on the Earth plane. There will be a new Earth energy that will elevate this one you are on to raise the frequency of all. The message is love, and love and acceptance should be the goal of all. I know you have felt alone here. You are not struggling; you have set up the life you needed to accomplish your mission to Earth. Everyone around you is here to do the same. The souls coming to Earth are to be heart-centered and release guilt and the brainwashing used for decades to keep people in fear. While in fear, you can't see the truth in a situation, story, or person."

I asked, "Is this the term 'blanketed'? I've been hearing this from God."

"Yes. When a person takes a blanket and places it on a birdcage, the bird cannot see and thinks it's time to sleep. That's what humanity has done to each other. The churches preach fire and brimstone, and many people have placed energetic hooks in the ones they say they love to shackle them to the fire-and-brimstone mentality. Think of how many people wouldn't get married if they weren't guilted and how many people wouldn't stay married if they felt they wouldn't be judged for following their own hearts. The men and women of Earth have been taught to put hooks into each other one way or another. These old ways are what's going to change."

I asked about certain situations that I had experienced growing up. I asked why my mom had to be so mean to me if I was here for a mission. She guided me back to the memory of my mother taking my first name away from me and explained that she acted out of fear for things she did not know how to handle. We talked about her answers in great detail, and I felt a calmness about her response to all I asked. She said she was going to leave, but she would be with me always. She was excited for me to find out exactly who I am and would wait patiently for me to do so as I continued to lift the veil of amnesia that had been placed on me through coming into the Earth plane.

When she left, I leaned back, relieved and exhausted as I sat there looking at the ceiling. I thought about how majestic she appeared and different from how I expected her to be with me. Even after seeing her and knowing she loved me, I still felt I was not good enough to have the name Mary. That wound had cut so deep, it still affected my most profound sense of identity.

***

The next morning when I got to the shop, C.J. said, "I can tell you didn't sleep."

"I was up reading and talking to Mother Mary," I explained. My answer frustrated her, and she began being rough with the merchandise she was pricing. As she continued talking to me, I could feel the anger welling up inside of her. *Why? Why is she so angry?* I felt God's frequency again, and this time, the message was clear. "She's afraid you're going to leave her." Her dark side was growing, as she knew I was beginning to ask questions for myself.

At that moment, Rodney walked in. He was one of our regulars and had suffered a terrible accident that left him only able to see auras but with no other abilities. He had a freaked-out look on his face when he looked at me. He asked C.J., "What the heck is wrong with her?"

C.J. glanced at me as if she couldn't care less and simply said, "She's going through a transition."

Rodney took a deeper look as he rotated around my body in awe. He looked deeper into my field, puzzled, saying, "I have never seen anything like that. Half of her energy field is blue, and the other half is purple. It is the strangest thing." He stood there watching me but seemed like he was trying to look away at the same time.

I noticed Archangel Michael's spirit come into the space. Archangel Michael stood at around nine feet tall, was fit, and had the most nonjudgmental energy. He looked like a bouncer at the most prestigious club anywhere, and no one could ever question his identity. His light was blue and white all at the same time, and his energy felt powerfully pure. As Rodney moved around the store collecting the items he needed, he still kept one eye on me. I could tell he didn't notice Archangel Michael; he couldn't even see him. I was beginning to wonder if C.J. could see him. She talked in her classes about channeling Archangel Michael and many others, yet she hadn't noticed him there.

Okay, I thought, *am I going crazy?* I tried to rationalize with myself. I suddenly remembered that people who are crazy never think that they are. I could tell by what C.J.'s energy showed she was still upset with me. The clock that hung in the back of the store showed me it was time to clock out. I picked up my purse from behind the counter, and I put some items on the counter for checkout. As she picked up the items one by one, she rang them up. At the same time, Archangel Michael moved behind me, and at that point, I was wondering how she could still not see him. *He's literally behind me!* I thought. She kept looking at me, then back at the items. When she finished ringing them all up, she set them into a bag and looked at me. *How can she still not see him?* At that point, I was nearly screaming the thoughts in my head. I heard God's frequency again, and that time he said, "Remember, she's blanketed."

After I paid her for the items, she said, "I really hope you stop communicating with the spirit side. You're spending too much time there, and it's affecting our relationship."

I took a deep breath, accepting the change I had to make, and said, "I really do appreciate everything that you've helped me with, especially the teachings and acceptance, but I think, at this point, it's better for me to just be on my own and figure things out. I know God has a plan for me, and I want to allow him to guide me."

She looked down at the counter and said, "Well, I've tried to warn you, and if you leave now, you'll never know what you can do or who you really are."

I could feel Archangel Michael's energy. At that point, it was as if his shield were around me and his sword drawn. I placed my hand on the door and slowly looked back at her. Before pushing the door open, I asked, "Do you see anyone here with us now?"

"Yes, Archangel Michael is with you," she said.

I heard God's voice say, "She can feel him, but she cannot see him." I took one last look at my friend, then turned and walked out the door.

Chapter Seven

The Glasses

Finally, the day came for my appointment with Julie Snow. As she entered my home, she paused at the threshold for a moment while looking at my energy field. We sat on the sofa, and she explained how she worked, then asked me a few questions. I had my massage table set up as she'd requested for the energy session. I lay down on the table, and she began by singing the Cherokee morning song. I recognized the song as the one Standing Eagle would sing when he did healing sessions. I don't recall what happened after that—I only remember waking up forty-five minutes later. Julie was standing over the table and looking at me with a smile. She sat down on the sofa and made some notes.

As she wrote, I noticed the medical symbol in her energy field. She saw me looking and said, "This is a habit from being a nurse for twenty-eight years." After she closed her bag, she asked, "Can I wait for the little boy who lives here?"

"Are you referring to Zach?" I asked.

She smiled and said, "Yes." While we waited, she told me about her classes and said that when I was ready, she would love to have me join.

The door opened, and Zach glided into the room. Julie's face lit up with happiness at seeing him. She patted the space next to her and said, "Come and sit next to Grandma Julie."

Zach loved conversations with strangers, as they gave him a chance to read their energy in his own way. Julie pointed down to his school bag and asked, "Is there a special book you're reading?" Zach gladly pulled a book from his bag and handed it to her. She said, "I'm going to teach you something you can do." Julie began by holding the book between her hands and closing her eyes. "You will say these words: 'Please show me all the information and pictures I need,'" she said. She waited a minute, then told him a short version of the book. She said, "It works best with thicker books without too many pictures." She glanced down to see my anatomy book on the floor next to the sofa. She picked up the book and placed it in his hands. The book was super thick for his hands, and he balanced it in his lap and repeated the words she spoke. As he held the book, I saw his eyelids flutter as pictures from the textbook ran through his mind.

He opened his eyes wide, amazed at the new trick Grandma Julie had taught him. Zach smiled and said, "I didn't finish because I needed to stop at the prostate." With a pained look on his face, he asked, "How long does it take to get through a book this thick?"

Julie explained, "The words you spoke were, 'Please show me all the information and pictures I need.'" She then explained that for thick books, it might take seven to ten minutes to download a book.

I had to ask, "Can I do this too?"

"You bet," Julie answered. She stood up and hugged and kissed Zach, telling him she would see him again. I hugged and thanked her for the session and lesson.

After she left, Zach asked, "What's for dinner?"

"Let's go to the bookstore at the mall. We can have dinner there and try out our newly discovered gift tonight on all the books we have wanted to read but couldn't afford," I answered. It was better than I could've imagined—we didn't even need to open the books; we just picked them up, placed them between our hands, and closed our eyes. A woman who worked there was walking around, restocking books. She glanced at us as if she was trying to make sure we weren't shoplifting. I felt it was time to go, and we left. The whole way home, Zach talked about how amazed he was by that new, quick way of reading. In the end, he said that his favorite way to read was still the old-fashioned way because it felt good to hold a book and turn pages.

The weekend came, and as we took a drive out to an old historical town, Zach and I noticed a fair. As we got closer, I could hear people laughing and cheering as unicyclists rode around. There were several tables set up, and each table had various signs for services being offered. Some of the services included tarot readings, palm readings, and aura photos, and there was even a caricature artist there. The fair was packed, and it seemed to be the most eclectic group of people I'd ever seen. Zach and I were taking in the scene when a lady greeted me and asked if we'd like to buy a raffle ticket.

"What's the raffle for?"

"Scarlett, of course!" she answered.

Who's Scarlett? Suddenly, the row of people blocking my view of Scarlett, who was standing twenty-five feet away, cleared, and a path opened. It seemed supernatural—as if God himself parted the way for me to see the energy around Scarlett. She was a blonde woman, probably ten years older than me. There was a sharp but connected edge at the top of her aura. The jagged aura wasn't common, and one side was more lopsided than the other over her head. The head region is known as the crown chakra. As I was taking a look at her, she zoned in on Zach and me. I could see that she was reading our energy. Someone was standing next to her and conversing as she was looking over. She walked away from the person without even excusing herself and came straight toward us. The person she'd been talking to looked confused. She glanced at me, then looked directly at Zach, bending down so she could be at his eye level. She looked as if she was honored to meet him and asked him for his autograph.

He smiled at her and said, "Okay."

She pulled a card with a pen from her pocket and handed them to him. He signed the card in his best six-year-old penmanship, then handed it back.

"Aren't you wondering why I wanted your autograph?" she asked, still unable to take her eyes off of him.

"Yes, why do you want my autograph?" he replied.

"You have a very unusual marking in your energy field. That marking is usually connected to somebody very famous," she told him. She turned to me and said, "Do you know which one I'm talking about? It's a blue mark above his head." She pointed it out while still focusing her eyes on Zach. She smiled and added, "I'll be the one who can say I got his autograph when he was little before he got famous."

"So, what do you do at the festival?" I asked.

She laughed and said, "I don't work at the festival," in a voice that led me to believe she thought it was beneath her. She explained that she saw auras and gathered what she needed to know in that way. I asked her to read my energy field. She said, "I have an office upstairs in this building. Let's go up there; there are too many people down here."

As I was following her lead and holding on to Zach, I felt the frequency say, "She needs to look at your field indoors to get a better look; the sunlight is too bright. In a room with less light, she can see better."

She guided us around back to what looked to be a secret entrance. A very narrow spiral staircase sat just inside the door, and up she went. Zach and I followed, and I could tell Zach was digging the secret space. The top of the stairs didn't have much of a landing. There were two rooms, and we entered the one that was not well lit. In fact, it barely had any light at all. I could tell Zach was in his own boy world, thinking about how some superheroes had secret hideouts and how that looked like a secret hideout too. She offered me a seat at a small table and told Zach to sit wherever he wanted. He happily plopped down on the sofa and got comfortable. I introduced myself as Katharine, and she said, "Funny—because on the way up the stairs, my guides told me your name is Mary." She proceeded to write "Mary" at the top of the page.

I put my hand over the name on the paper and said in a very firm voice while looking into her eyes, "Call me Katharine."

She nodded in acknowledgment but didn't change the name on the page as she began to sketch a drawing of me and my energy field. I heard the frequency say she had been in a horrible accident and almost died. My eyes were directed to observe the scar on her forehead. She then said, "I know you see colors around the body—what else do you see?"

I quickly froze, as I didn't expect her to care about what I saw, and I didn't know what to say. I explained to her that I looked into the body and that I saw conception to death.

She continued to perfect her illustration of my field, then invited me to come to a psychometry workshop Tuesday night. She wrote a note on the paper, then folded it for me. I picked up my purse and reached in for my wallet. Noticing, she said, "Come to the class, and we'll call it even. Bring a friend if you'd like."

Zach knew it was time to go and stood up, moving toward the door we'd come in through. "Let's go out the front," she said as she revealed a door by moving what we thought were just curtains. She opened it, and Zach was amazed that there was another exit to the room. It was a surefire way to pique his curiosity and his adventurous side.

***

When Tuesday came around, I had almost forgotten about the invitation to Scarlett's class. I didn't feel like I should bring Zach, but I didn't want to go alone. I invited my friend Angel to the class—after all, Scarlett said I could bring someone. I knew when too many spirits would come in to communicate at once, I usually panicked. Too many spirits, in my case, meant a few hundred. I didn't want to worry about how I was going to drive in case that happened at the class. Having Angel with me would alleviate the worry of getting home.

Angel picked me up, and we headed to the class. He voiced his concerns about me going into the old historical home where the class was being held. Angel was great at noticing my tell when I became too immersed in another dimension right before a panic attack. I didn't realize when my tell was apparent. Others didn't usually know what was happening either, because to them, I just looked like a person watching an interesting show on television. At those moments, I'd lose myself, forgetting I was okay and alive in the moment and that everything was fine. Being reminded of that was the first thing I needed to hear to get me back here and out of the dimension I was peering into.

It was completely dark outside when we pulled up, except for one very visible sign that said "Ghost Tours Nightly" along with a few people hanging around outside on the porch. Angel looked at the house and said, "This is a spooky-looking place; no wonder they do ghost tours here." Just before exiting the car, he threw out a code word for us to say if we needed to leave.

When we got inside, everyone was acting like they were very attuned, and some were bragging about what they could see. I noticed a couple of people looking at us as if we were out of place. Angel and I didn't talk much, not even to each other, as we walked through the shop in the front of the house loaded with crystals and spiritual objects. It was nothing I hadn't already seen in C.J.'s shop.

When Scarlett was ready for the class, she asked everyone to sit at a long conference table. There were twelve people, including Scarlett. The lights were low, and a big bowl of chocolates sat in the center. Scarlett removed the chocolates, placed them on a side table, and told us that if anyone began to feel spacey to help themselves. She then pulled up a large empty bowl and placed it on the table. She began by saying, "When you all signed up for the class, I asked you to bring something that you could allow another to read by psychometry." I thought back to the day she invited me, and in no way did she mention bringing an item.

"This is great; I have something," Angel said, leaning in.

I didn't have anything with me other than the locket around my neck that belonged to Grammy. As Scarlett began to pass the bowl, she said, "Put your item in and don't let anyone see it." As the bowl was coming around to me, I tried to undo the clasp of the necklace I was wearing, and she said, "No, I have something I would like you to read." Scarlett's energy seemed confident as if she had planned that on the day we met. Once everyone's item was loaded into the bowl, she passed it to the lady on my right and asked her to draw one item while not looking. She said, "Please hold the item and pass the bowl." Once everyone had an object in their hand and was holding it to see what they were picking up on, she set a timer for five minutes.

As I was sitting empty-handed, the frequency came in. I heard it say, "She has something else for you to hold." My hands were clasped together in the prayer position under the table as I began to think about that code word Angel mentioned. When I glanced at Angel, he was holding the item he had drawn from the bowl, and his eyes were closed. I noticed that one of the women who had given us her backstory and praises before class was sitting there with an orange energy field. *Wait a minute*, I thought. *Orange is fear, so what is it that she fears right now?* The time was up for those trying to pick up vibrations from the objects. Scarlett started with the woman to my right named Carla. She began to give descriptive words about the previous owner of the item. All the things said were complimentary. She finished in two minutes, though part of the two minutes was her saying her name and how long she had been working as a psychic. After she shared, the object was claimed by the owner.

Angel was next. I loved having him as my friend; he was the most honest, loving, and humble person I'd ever met. He held up his item and said, "I don't understand the spiritual stuff, but when I held this, I felt that the person who had it had a life of struggle, and this object represented to its owner success in making a life here in the United States."

The man on the end of the table said, "That's right, it belonged to my grandfather, and he saw that as his lucky pocket piece." As the bowl went around the table, everyone had a turn.

When all the items were complete, Scarlett looked at one of the women sitting at the table. "Please give her the glasses," she said while motioning to me. The woman took out a pair of regular eyeglasses and set them on the table. Scarlett turned to me and said, "When you pick up the glasses, I want you to immediately share the message you receive and the feeling you get from holding them."

I picked the glasses up, and within a couple of seconds, I felt as if I were running and became out of breath even though I was sitting still. As I was feeling breathless, I began to describe each sensation. I suddenly felt a knife go into my back and had the feeling of falling forward to the ground. The weight of a man was on my back. At that moment, I felt fluids moving throughout my body in places where they shouldn't. As I felt I was still on the ground, the knife went into my back again and again. Suddenly, there was a bright light, and I could smell the scent of gardenias. Saint Francis stepped forward and said, "She is not here; the owner of those glasses spent a short time here then reincarnated."

I leaned back in my chair, as I had never felt something so horrible from merely holding an object. The woman who'd handed me the glasses was in tears, and Scarlett looked around the room and said, "That's exactly what happened to the owner of those glasses." I handed them back to the woman, and she explained it was her sister who was killed sixteen years before by her soon-to-be ex-husband. She told us she had carried those glasses to other classes and to many psychics, and they never told her what I did. She thanked Scarlett. Scarlett had told her to come that night because when she met me, she thought she had found the one who would see what needed to be seen. Hearing that her sister had been reincarnated after her tragic and violent death gave the woman the peace she had been seeking.

I just wanted to get out of there and go take a shower. As Angel was talking about the amazing evening, I completely zoned out. Even when he dropped me off, I was left with more questions than I started with. I wondered, *Why was I able to see and feel things that the victim's sister couldn't feel for herself*? Once again, I was in contemplation on why others were not seeing what I was seeing.

***

In the late fall of 2007, I attended an energy healing class. Prior to class, I hadn't met anyone who would be there except the instructor. We all took turns introducing ourselves and providing a brief explanation about why we decided to attend. I could feel someone staring at me with a hard focus. The woman across from me introduced herself, and as I listened, I saw the spirit of a man in his mid-twenties standing behind her. She explained that the class was important to her because she wanted to help others who may have gone through a traumatic situation or grief. The man standing behind her began to smile, as he knew I could see him. He mentally told me he was her son.

When she was finished, I told her that there was a man between twenty-four and twenty-six, big smile and handsome, who said he was her son.

She reached across the table and touched my arm, saying, "That's my son, Kevin," while thanking me for letting her know. She explained that she knew he was with her and that she wanted to be able to talk to him. He'd been killed in a motorcycle accident, and she missed him.

After class, we all exchanged business cards before leaving. As I cruised home, the freeway was void of cars. It was a Tuesday night, so that seemed normal for 10:00 p.m. The radio was playing great songs, one right after another. As I was singing "Hey Soul Sister" right along with Train—which was probably my best singing ever—I noticed my exit coming up. I glanced in my rearview mirror to check that all lanes were clear, and as I did, I saw Kevin in the back seat, laughing at me. After exiting, I glanced back while trying to avoid the cement esplanade, and he was gone.

As I pulled into the drive, I felt it wouldn't be the last time he would visit now that he knew I could see and hear him.

The house was dark, and when I felt around and flipped on the light switch, Kevin was there. He said, "You need to call my mom—I need you to convey a few messages that are important."

I was feeling squeamish and cold while trying to explain that I didn't really know his mom. He moved forward and said, "You have her business card, so you can call her in the morning." I knew he wouldn't leave me alone until I did, so I quickly agreed.

The next morning while I lay in bed, trying to open my eyes, the sun shone through a small slit in the curtains with a blinding aggravation. I got up and walked out to the living room, thinking about the night before as I caught a glimpse of the business card hanging halfway off the coffee table. I felt relieved that Kevin hadn't visited yet, but just as soon as I had that thought, he appeared on the sofa, motioning for me to come and sit. "Can you call her now?" he asked.

I picked up the phone, and with great anxiety, I dialed her number. Just as I was wishing for the call to go to voicemail, she answered. I reminded her of our meeting the previous night and told her, "Kevin is here and would like me to communicate with him now. Is that okay?"

I could hear her suck in air as if she couldn't get her words out, then I finally heard her say yes. I knew her reply was accompanied by soft tears. Kevin began to explain that he knew she'd hired a private investigator, and he wanted her to cancel the investigation. She said she was told by his best friend that he helped father a child. He said that was correct, that it was a friend from high school who was married, and she and her husband couldn't conceive. The husband didn't know about the agreement she'd made with Kevin. He only knew they'd finally become pregnant after years of heartbreak. "I donated sperm so they could have a child, and that child has two parents who love her. If you get involved, this child will be raised without a father, and that was not the plan." She agreed, explaining she had hoped to be able to hang on to part of him.

He leaned in and clarified that the relationship between him and his mom was never good, and that's why he left when he turned eighteen. As I could hear her crying with tears of guilt, I hoped he would say something good—something reassuring. He said, "The struggle was our earthly connection. It was the relationship we needed to have so we could go on and do other things. You now want to help others and learn about spiritual stuff when before, the thick Bible on our bookshelf was never opened. It was my loss that brought you to want to evolve and achieve the path you set out to accomplish while you are on Earth. The other thing I need you to do is stop looking to buy a Ouija board. The spirits who communicate through it are not in the light. They are disincarnated spirits who are stuck, and they are not good. So get rid of that makeshift thing you have on the table."

She laughed as if she'd been caught doing something wrong—but not too wrong—and I could feel a sheepish grin come across her face. She said she'd bought a vinyl tablecloth and was drawing a Ouija board across the top. He laughed and told her to throw it out.

She asked in a pleading voice, "When will I be able to hear you?"

"You will in about two months." There were things he needed to learn, and he needed time to build up his light body since, before the accident, he had weakened it by doing drugs.

I was suddenly feeling way too close to the pair and wanted it to end with an "I love you." *Please*, I thought, praying in my head. *Say I love you.* Just as I thought it, Kevin said, "I love you, Mom," and she began crying again with happy tears of gratitude. I thanked them both for allowing me to have the opportunity to witness their interaction since I learned a few things I had not witnessed before. As soon as the call was over, Kevin waved while disappearing through the portal he must have come through. I felt it was not going to be the last time I'd see him.

***

A year had gone by when I was working on someone who requested Reiki. We discussed the items she wanted to work on, and she began to explain that she'd had work done by someone else who was very good. It was wonderful when a person found an energy healer they worked well with, so I asked why she had come to me instead. She explained that she'd had a very odd experience that left her feeling freaked out. The healer kept talking of her deceased son during the energy work and how he came in and told her where she needed to focus the energy. I began to zone out as she gave examples of things the woman told her, as I knew who she was talking about.

Later that evening, as I was climbing into bed and thinking about that conversation, Kevin came in. His energy field looked much brighter than it had previously, and I recalled the work he'd needed to do to build up his light body. He sat on what appeared to be the same height as the bed, but nothing was under him; he was about a foot and half from the edge and seemed comfortable. He laughed with a cute smirk and made fun of the fact that I never seemed shocked to see him. Trying some spirit humor, I asked if anyone ever jumped out of their skin when they saw him. He said not many adults could see him, and the ones who did couldn't hear him. I was taking mental notes for my own learning and understanding. As he sat quietly, I knew the conversation was going to result in another plea to call his mom. I shook my head while saying, "No."

"Why no?" he said.

"Your mom can hear you; you've been helping her with healing. I just had someone today tell me she had a session with your mom, and she explained how you've been guiding her to where she needs to work on the person."

He said, "That's true; we've begun to communicate. She loves the gift of knowing where the client needs energy sent. But it has to stop. The communication was a way to help her in grieving so she could release the guilt around our earthly relationship. It's time for her to tune in to higher-level spirits and ask the spirit guides and angels for help. It's time for me to reincarnate to my next life, but as long as she keeps calling on me, it's holding me back."

I asked him to explain, reminding him I was learning some of it fresh and new.

"The only way to explain it is to think about yourself on a trip flying halfway around the world, and as you reach nine hours into your flight, the pilot gets on the speaker and says he's turning the plane around and flying back."

I considered that. Trying to invoke humor, I said, "I guess the passengers would be mad."

"You bet. Imagine you'd invested nine hours, plus the work that was done to prepare for the flight, not to mention dealing with the babies crying from their little ears drums popping and the guy who didn't shower prior to running to make the flight and the woman who fell asleep and was crowding your space."

I smiled and told him, "I understand; it would be annoying."

"When people pray or talk to loved ones," he explained, "it is beautiful, but she has built her practice on calling me every day while I have things I want to be doing on the other side. This life is one of many I plan to live and incarnate in."

My guidance from the frequency was that he needed to tell her himself—it was not a message that would be well received from me. I told him I was grateful for all he had shared and taught me, but I should not be the one to deliver the message. If he explained it to her, she could teach the information to others. I could feel love from him as his spirit accepted my explanation.

"What are you planning to do in your next life?" I asked.

He told me he was going to be a spiritual arborist. He had already met up with another spirit who planned to incarnate in the same timeline so they could be together. He had not been with her in two hundred years. I could see the happiness in his soul's color and considered how different he was from when I first met him. Even now, when I hear Train's "Hey, Soul Sister," I think of his big grin in the rearview mirror.

The interaction with Kevin taught me so much about what the deceased know on the other side and the limits to what they don't know. His spirit displayed the same sense of humor he'd had in the life he'd just left; it was an identifying trait to his true soul. So many people think if a relative has a bad temper or is a mean person, that is the way they will always be, even on the other side. My interactions with Kevin showed me that isn't always how it works—our spirits retain our personality, but we can continue to grow and develop. I've encountered souls who were very bitter and passive-aggressive while they walked the earth who didn't show that in the communication I had with them after they passed. In fact, those were things they were disappointed in about how they'd showed up in this life when they were alive. After death, all lower energetic emotions evaporate, leaving the human experiences and behaviors on the Earth plane.

***

In order to explain my limited scope of the world, I should mention that ever since I was an adult, I have chosen to be decade impaired. What does that mean? It means that I never watch TV shows and movies except those from the 1970s and 1980s. That was all I would let my kids see too. It was easy to do most of the time when they were young. We didn't have cable—we didn't even have regular TV—and I was never one to watch the news. There were a few times the kids and I would show up at the grocery store to shop, and everyone was running around like ants, throwing things into their baskets. When I stopped someone to ask what was going on, they told me there was a hurricane coming. I had no idea what was happening in the world, and I loved it that way. My secret talent was knowing every lyric to old TV show theme songs. *The Brady Bunch*, *Good Times*, *WKRP in Cincinnati*, and *The Jeffersons* were some of my favorites.

Christmas was approaching, and while everyone was making plans with extended family, my primary focus was Breezy and Zach. Every Christmas Eve, we would go to Macaroni Grill and then to the movies. It was great—the theater was always empty except for the three of us and maybe one or two other people. Our family picture would be from the photo booth. We would go home, open a gift, and have an enjoyable evening together. The next day, we would open the rest of the presents, cook, and watch movies. My biological family would get together either at my sister's or brother's house and celebrate with Mom and my stepdad.

That particular year, my anxiety was at the point where even being around my family would've been too stressful. Besides, I knew they didn't understand what I did, and it would've been too difficult to convince them of the value of my work. I realized their approval wasn't important for my clients or for me. Often, our family members fail to recognize the changes we've made and never wish to see us as better than the perception in their minds. When I talked to Mom, she would mention that other family members had asked about me or missed me, which I felt was only partially true. Their "pity shower" toward me was way too thick, and while their intentions might have been good, their judgment was crippling their own spiritual growth—not mine. The frequency had guided me that holding judgment rather than accepting was an underlying problem for humanity.

I had recently acquired a new client who found me through a friend. She bought a one-hour session with me and asked a string of questions that were not psychic questions; they were only questions about me and how long I've been doing the job. Before we got off the phone, she booked another session for the following day, telling me that session would be different than the one we'd just had. When we got off the phone, I felt a breeze, but it wasn't a breeze that I would feel where I was in Texas; it was a breeze in Santa Monica, California.

After the call, my spirit guide informed me I was the person the woman had been looking for. From the questions she asked, at some point in the reading, she must have realized I didn't know many actors by name or face. The next day she called me and said, "I have someone here who would like to ask you a few questions."

When she handed the phone over to her friend, I was nervous; then I heard a familiar voice. As I began to read the frequency, I saw a vision of her friend from the night before at his home while he was suffering a panic attack. I told him what I was seeing and that I was an expert on panic attacks and knew what needed to be done.

I had a couple of clients who were writers and directors. My contact information had been passed around, so I was reading for many other people in the film industry. Sometimes they'd mention their projects, but they knew I couldn't reference any of their shows, movies, or plays since I was decades behind the times. I hadn't seen anything that was currently popular. That might have been what they liked best about working with me since no one was getting special treatment. Other people would hold back to stay in good with them, but I told them what I would see without reservation. I didn't care if I was talking to a famous person or someone down the street from me, so long as I was getting paid for readings. Integrity was important, and I would be doing them a disservice if I condoned anything that was not the highest and best on their spiritual path. As I've said before, when the universe wants us to learn something, it will be shown to us, and we can bank that information, as we will use and reflect on it later.

I got a call from a guy named Randel who needed me to look into a case that had been bothering him. He was looking to get a law put into effect to prevent the situation from happening again. We met at one of my usual lunch spots, and as we were being taken to the table, there was a spirit of a woman there. She was tall, she looked to be around twenty-five years old, and she was glowing. She looked like she was wearing clothes from the 1950s and seemed happy to see me. *Ah*, I thought, *she must be here for Randel*. We sat down, and I was trying not to look weird since I knew Randel was trying to size me up as he'd intuitively done throughout his long legal career. He pulled out a folder and showed me a photo of a woman. He told me her name was Linda Rogers, and he believed she was murdered. As I took the photo into my hand, the woman who was present in spirit pointed to the photo and told me that it was her.

"So you're Linda?" I asked her.

"Yes," she replied.

I asked him what he wanted to know about Linda, explaining that the woman in the photo was seventy-eight, but the spirit who was present was in her mid-twenties. He smiled and said he was familiar with spirits choosing a younger age after they crossed.

As Linda looked at the photo, she commented, *That body was tired and was not treated well.* I explained to Randel that I'd listen to his spirit guides, his angels, and the person he wished to talk to, then I'd parrot what they said to me. I pulled out a pad of paper and had it ready in the event his spirit guides wanted me to write. Linda was very pleasant to talk to, and as I was reading, she told me she liked the bracelets on my wrist. I had several on that day, but she seemed drawn to the one with the infinity symbol. Randel seemed happy after the session. He was a big help in my career, and so was Linda, as she was the one who gave the answers. He continued sending me clients for several years. Linda's details became helpful with future cases because of similarities. Also, there was a karmic tit for tat lesson that I learned about in Linda's untimely death.

Back at home, there was a message taped to the front door that read, "I came by to see if you could give me a session. You don't know me yet, but I've heard good things about you. Signed, Hollywood." *Hollywood?* I thought. *This is ridiculous.* Before I could get my phone out to call him back, one of my neighbors came around the front and said that a big car had pulled up a while ago.

"Did you see the person?" I asked.

"Only from the side view and from thirty feet away."

I called the number back, and he insisted that I meet him at the hotel he was staying at. He told me to go straight to the front desk and let them know I was looking for Hollywood. As I approached the front desk, I looked at the energy fields of the girls behind it, and I could tell some of them were wondering what I did for work. By their energy, they seemed intrigued by what Hollywood could want from me. I gave them my name and told them I was looking for Hollywood. One of them came out from behind the counter and asked me to follow her. She took me to a private dining room attached to the hotel restaurant.

The walls were glass from ceiling to floor. It was very elegant, and there was a long buffet table set up with all kinds of food and a round table set for dinner with a man sitting behind it. When I walked in, he stood up and put his hand out to greet me. He told me he was in Houston for business, and my name was mentioned to him by a friend. It was weird when he said "friend" because it didn't seem to sit right. He offered me a chair and asked if I was hungry. I asked what type of reading he was looking for, as I could see many indiscretions of varying degrees in his energy field. It was a two-hour reading. I gave him all the notes from my automatic writing and the illustrations of certain things that I saw about projects he would begin soon.

"You could make a lot of money in California if you decide to move. Be sure to let me know. It may be beneficial since you have a good client base built there already," he said as he handed me a business card. I knew he was more intrigued with me than I was with him.

Work was steady, and as things began to get better and better, I realized I could say no to certain clients. So when someone requested a session, if I felt I wouldn't be a good fit for them or they weren't ready to walk their spiritual path, I would simply refer them to someone else. I was at the point of not wanting to take a session just to take a session. I really wanted to help those who sought to awaken and walk their spiritual path and those who were truly ready to forsake anything that could hinder that process.

It had been a couple of months since I read for Hollywood when I got a call from him. He said he wanted to fly me out to California for his Christmas party. "I know my guests would get a kick out of you," he added.

"That sounds great. What's the attire? Black tie?" I asked.

"Yes, but I want you to dress like a gypsy," he said.

"Dress like a gypsy—so it's a costume party?" I asked.

"No," he said, "you're doing readings for the party, so I want you to look the part."

"Listen, Hollywood, I don't think I'm the girl for the job. I don't dress like a gypsy normally, so why would I do it for a party? Let me give you the number of someone I know who would love to do this," I said.

"Okay. Does she have dark hair and dark features like you?" he inquired.

A month and a half later, Hollywood contacted me for a reading. I told him I had a full day and was heading to lunch. When I was about to order, I noticed him walking into the restaurant with a big smile because he'd managed to find me. "Please, eat your lunch; I'm going to get something," he said upon greeting me. His behavior was so presumptuous—it was my lunch break, and he hadn't scheduled an appointment. "Since I was able to join you, we can have a session while I eat," he said with a grin.

Reluctantly, I read for him. When we got ready to leave, he was standing about a foot and a half from me, and as I went to pick up my purse, he leaned in and shoved his right hand down the front of my pants, at the same time trying to kiss me. I yanked his arm out and pushed him away.

He looked at me in shock and said, "I'm in love with who you are and what you do."

"Well I'm not interested in you!" I said and left.

The next day, a courier service knocked on the door and asked me to sign for a delivery. As I opened the box, I saw a bracelet from a jeweler in Houston and a handwritten note card with an apology that was signed, "Love, Hollywood."

Chapter Eight

The House

I received a call from Julie Snow inviting me to attend her weekend energy class. It was going to be held for two days at a beautiful resort that was usually used for yoga and counseling retreats. It seemed like a unique opportunity because it was an ongoing class that would be held one weekend per month for a whole year.

When I got there, I received a warm welcome from Julie. The others who were there seemed as if they were forming cliques already. There were ten students altogether. Julie had us sit in a circle on the floor and go around and introduce ourselves using nicknames. If we had a name that started with the letter B, we had to come up with a nickname that started with the letter B. After everyone went around the room, she explained that we should put the nicknames in front of our real names. She said it would make it much easier for us to remember each other. Everyone seemed to have fun with it, and there was lots of laughter and teasing. I went to the restroom for a tinkle break, and while I was gone, she asked everyone to pair up with a partner. When I came back, Pop-Tart Paul was standing there alone, and Julie said, "You'll be partners."

There were five massage tables set up. Julie asked everyone to pick a table and have one person lie down while their partner stood next to the table and ran their hands up and down the body, searching for warm spots that indicated which areas needed to be worked on. By then, I could hear the thoughts of several of the women who were glad Pop-Tart Paul was not their partner.

I'm sure if they had known the intent of the name game, most would have selected a different nickname. Some of them were still laughing about the choice they had made. I knew where the name game was going, so I said Kitty, and they had to call me Kitty Kat. Junkyard Julie and Bottoms-up Brenda didn't fare so well.

As Pop-Tart stood next to the table, I asked him to turn. Glancing at his body, I could see exactly what was happening on the inside and outside. I was also able to see some of the injuries his body had incurred over the years. Julie urged us to begin talking to our partners about what we found within the energy field. As Pop-Tart and I began chatting, I told him what I saw within his body. I explained the injuries he had and the ages he was when they happened. He was impressed. Sure, most of the people in the class had silly nicknames, but the group was composed of several very professional people, including a couple of doctors who simply wanted to take the class to add to what they did. Pop-Tart was a clinical psychologist. Julie walked around the tables, talking to each partner and asking if they had succeeded in finding the trouble spots and confirming with their partners. When Julie walked over to our table, Pop-Tart was still very much in awe over what I'd told him. We were the last table she walked over to, so at that point, all the other students were listening to what Julie was saying to Pop-Tart and me. I could tell Julie was about to teach me a lesson. She said, "Show me how you scanned his body with your hands." That was how she told us to do it, but I didn't need to do it that way because

I could already see into his body. I saw all of his major injuries that had occurred after his conception to the ones that would happen in the future up to the time of his death. It was only important for me to note the injuries he had in the past and the ones he had at that moment in time. That's why I shared those findings with Pop-Tart. The other people in the class who had brushed me off and snubbed me when I arrived were suddenly intrigued.

Julie wasn't going to let me off easy. "Take your hands and run them up and down his body to feel for the spots you need to work on," she commanded.

I thought to myself, *I can see way more with my perception than anyone could feel with their hands.* Running one's hands up and down someone's body to feel for spots doesn't mean touching them. I hadn't avoided using Julie's technique because I wanted to remain hands-off—remaining hands-off was part of her suggested technique anyway. It was just that I knew an easier way. Pop-Tart was really impressed, but Julie was pissed.

I finished the class that weekend and decided I didn't want to go back for any of the other weekends. It wasn't something I wanted to spend my time doing since it would take up one weekend each month for eleven more months. Besides, I didn't feel like I needed to be reprimanded that way. It would've been a perfect opportunity for her to use what I saw, then ask everyone else to come in and do the energy work that needed to be done.

Some people took the course that Julie offered so that they could have their own energy practice. Some of them were just looking to incorporate it into what they were already doing for work. Julie was very attuned to herself and to the human body. She knew a lot and had studied under Barbara Brennan. I learned some things from her, like how to recognize that everyone has a superpower and that there's no right or wrong way to receive a message. Julie's practice had been steady; she was awesome with her superpower as a healer. Even though continuing her class wasn't right for me, I was grateful I had learned what I needed to from her.

My business was coming from word of mouth and from the site traffic on a psychic hotline I worked for. People were throwing money at me, wanting more sessions. I was hoping they wouldn't need to come in weekly. I thought that doing a few sessions would get clients to want to walk an enlightened path in whatever they chose to do. There's not an occupation that couldn't benefit from learning to tune in to one's own spiritual gifts. That's what I believe our psychic perception was meant for—everyday use. Everyone would be able to use it if they would allow themselves to tune in. Yet, the majority of people are walking around with their senses muted. I had realized at that point that our senses became muted by trauma and emotional and physical abuse. The food we consume and the way we choose to live play a part in it as well.

The next couple of weeks became very interesting. I had a slew of new clients who all had issues with erectile dysfunction. As I've mentioned, I had begun to notice a pattern. The pattern was that when the universe wanted me to learn something, it sent it to me more than once, and if I didn't get it, I was sent yet more chances to learn. As I began the sessions, there was one underlying cause that was the primary reason behind the issue in my clients: it was marijuana. Most of the guys I'd been reading for were in their mid-twenties. The oldest was thirty-one years old. They had all smoked pot, and a few had been smoking daily. After I compiled all of the notes that I'd been taking to do my study of what was happening to these individuals, I was shown a thin, see-through blanket of film being laid over their entire energy fields. Pot was not only stifling their ability to engage the way they wanted to, but it was also slowing their spiritual awakening. The frequency came in and explained that marijuana was not intended for the overuse that is popular. It was only intended for one small leaf to be used as a treatment for various ailments. The marijuana plant itself had been altered several times since its beginning, and the alterations were doing the human body more harm than good. I was then shown that several different variations of the drug were a cause of growth in male breast tissue, erectile dysfunction, and depression in both males and females. It took around six months for the energy field to clear after stopping its use.

***

My days were becoming blurred together, as all I could focus on was working every single hour possible. It was important to me so I could buy a house and get us out of the apartment complex we had been living in. The apartment was nice. We lived near the waterway, and it was a short walk to the movie theater and mall. But it was difficult to relax being so close to the other residents' energy fields. I had to keep reminding myself that living in the apartment was just temporary.

I worked seven days a week from 7:30 a.m. to 8:30 p.m. As my skills improved, I could tell a shift in my gifts was happening. I had somehow managed to listen to what deceased spirits were saying and showing me while remaining face-to-face with another person in conversation. It was not something I tried to do. One day, I noticed it happening while talking to a neighbor.

All of the neighbors were nice, helpful, good people except for the guys in one apartment. Two guys lived there: Mark and Sean.

One afternoon, I was out front waiting for Zach to get home from school. I could see Mark trying to size me up from a distance. Then he walked up to me. He stumbled around, trying to ask if we could talk. He said the neighbors had told him what I could see and asked if I would answer something for him.

I didn't want any trouble and thought, *What could be wrong with answering one question*? He told me he had a lot of guilt about not seeing his cousin before she passed. At that moment, the cousin's spirit stepped forward, and she was in full light form, which showed me that she went into the light. She appeared to me as a teenager, with wispy brown hair and an angelic face. Then I had a vision of the life she had recently left. She'd been confined to a bed and wheelchair and was unable to speak. Then she showed me that Mark would sexually molest her when he visited. She said, "This is what he wants forgiveness from." There was no anger from her, only pity since he was given an Earth experience, yet he was using it for deviant acts. As I refocused on what Mark was saying, I knew I couldn't just tell him he was disgusting. It's up to the individual to find the need to change to make the human experience what it was meant for: soul perfection. I quickly ended the conversation, as I knew my time would be wasted on someone who would not change.

***

That night, I prayed for God to guide me to the perfect house for the kids and me, and I was open to whatever I needed to know. Over the next two weeks, I worked on staying focused while keeping my kids busy. There was a colony of feral cats we were feeding behind the apartments. They lived between the rear of the apartments that backed up to a park. I would buy a twenty-pound bag of food per week, and we would feed them every night. While I had nice neighbors, I knew the ones who didn't know me thought I was strange. It was probably a mix of knowing what I did for a living and my appearance. Some people who don't understand automatically think my work is all witchcraft. I'm definitely not a witch, but they didn't know the difference, so they labeled me out of ignorance.

It was Saturday morning. I normally got up earlier on Saturdays so I could get started with the weekend callers. My work desk was conveniently placed in front of the large window of my bedroom so I could sit and look out as I worked. I noticed there were several black vans outside that day. I could tell some kind of an arrest was happening. After the vans cleared away, one of my neighbors knocked on my door. She said the police came and arrested Mark and Sean. From what she'd learned, they were suspected pedophiles. I was so grateful that the police actually got those guys. I was unaware of what they were doing because I don't walk around reading everyone, but after that one vision of his cousin, I was glad that they were caught.

The following week, the complex had everything removed from their office and taken out to the dumpster. They quickly leased the place to a young couple with a toddler. When I saw the wife, I knew she was vengeful. It was gross thinking about the two guys who lived in the apartment before, knowing now there was a couple living there with their young child. It gave me more inspiration to get out of the complex.

After a month had gone by, I was ready to buy a house. I found a realtor and told him exactly what I was looking for. When I was ready to go look at houses, I told him I didn't have a lot of time to go out and look and that I trusted God to bring me to the right one. "Follow the parameters I'm giving you and just show me the house that comes up,"

I told him. I felt like I was giving him a wide range of opportunities to find me the right place.

That night as I was closing down for bed, I asked God to please make it obvious which house we were supposed to move into so that I could make the right choice. At that moment, I saw Jesus's face. I asked him, "Do you have any information about the house I'm supposed to move to?" He smiled but didn't say anything. I just knew that I would have the house I needed. That night, I went to sleep and dreamt that a beautiful lotus flower opened up. From inside the lotus came a lovely fairy. The fairy looked at me and said, "Do you see the house behind me? This is your house." I awoke feeling happy.

The weekend came around, and we went to look at the places my realtor found. I noticed they seemed far off from what I wanted. After the third house, I told him none of the houses were right. "Show me the houses closest to Market Street," I reiterated.

"Okay, look, there's a house close to Market Street, and it's exactly what you want, but it needs a lot of work. If you'd like, you can follow me over there," he said.

We followed him in our car, and when we pulled up, the front of the house was basically covered in trees. We were all standing in front, and the realtor was holding a flyer in his hand. He told me when the house was built and gave me the stats. I asked him what the address was. The realtor looked down at the paperwork, looked back at the house, and said, "Seven."

Seven? Wow—seven is Jesus's number. I turned to him and said, "What's the name of the street?"

"Glorybower."

Everything is being divinely calculated, I thought. *The number seven is Jesus's number. Glorybower—glory means the glory of God.*

I must've stood there looking at him in silence for too long because he said, "Glorybower, you know, bowing to the glory!"

I glanced over the house and noticed there were some numbers by the door. They were 007. I laughed and thought, *Someone was living out their double-oh-seven fantasy here.*

"Would you like to look at the house? It's way under the price range you were looking for. I just didn't think this was your style."

I glanced over and told him, "I want to put a contract on it." I knew the house was meant for me. As I stood there looking at it, I heard God's voice say, "In no time at all, this house will be worth five times more than what you're paying for it at this moment."

The realtor turned to me in complete shock and said, "I've only shown you three houses. This is the fourth house—most people like to look at several homes, compare comps, and negotiate before they make a choice. Are you sure about this?"

I could tell he had real concern for me buying the house, not feeling like it was the right one for me, and not ever having had that experience with another buyer before. I said, "I'm positive I want to buy this house."

"Let me at least show you the inside."

We walked in and saw a spiral staircase. As we went up into the master bedroom, there was a balcony. I had always thought I'd like to have a balcony off the bedroom. The house had a very good vibration. The realtor told me he would drop off all the paperwork and handed me the pages with the photos of the house so I would have them. I glanced at the photos, and several of them had orbs. I knew it was a good house with good energy. We just needed our offer to be accepted, and we could move out of the apartment.

To celebrate the fact that we had found a home, we went out for dinner. It was quite cloudy that day, so I knew we would have rain. It felt good going back to the apartment knowing we wouldn't have to live there for much longer.

We would normally venture out at eight every evening to feed the cat colony. That particular evening, I could hear thunder coming, so I wanted to get the food to them before eight. As Zach and I stepped out onto the sidewalk, I could feel eyes on us. We walked behind the building where no one could see and began putting the food out. When we came back around to the front of our place, a woman was peering down from the third-floor balcony. The wind had picked up at that point. Thunder rolled across the sky, and my hair was blowing in every direction. As I glanced up, our eyes met. I heard God say she was a spiteful person and not to trust her.

The next morning, when we left for school, there was a notice on the front door from the office of the apartments. It read, "It's been brought to our attention that you have been feeding stray cats. The cats are making so much noise screaming and crying that it's keeping one of the residents up."

I knew that was an outright lie, as no one else would know the cats were there. They didn't make a peep; they didn't even fight with each other. I sat there and cried, thinking about the cats and how I was going to get food for them. *How can someone's heart be so mean? It's not costing her anything for me to feed them.* As I cried, I heard God's voice say there would be remorse on her part for doing that, as she had a tough road ahead of her.

The realtor informed me that our offer was accepted. I was feeling so happy, I got into the car and drove over to the house to take a look. When I pulled up, I was told to go to the front. When I got there, the frequency came in and said to look. *Okay, so what am I looking at?* As I tuned in to listen, I was guided to the front door. It had a screen door that had seen better days. I was told to open the screen, and as I did,

I saw the lotus flower that the fairy had shown me. It was a gold lotus flower in the glass of the door. *How did I miss this when I came with the realtor?*

"You were too busy looking at the house to see the detail."

I thought, *The first thing I'm going to do is get the screen door off and paint the house and smile every time I see the lotus.*

***

Zach and Breezy needed school supplies. As we were getting in the car to go shopping, I heard a gunshot. I looked at Zach and said, "Did you hear that sound?"

"Yes."

I said, "That was a gunshot."

For some reason, I felt the gunshot was louder for me as part of a spiritual lesson. I didn't know what, and at that very moment, it was something that was going to have to wait. I needed to hurry over to Target and get school supplies.

Coming back from Target, as I entered the neighborhood, I could see the spirit of a man standing on the corner. It felt weird to me, but I drove past him and turned onto my street. The next few days, every time I left the neighborhood, he would be out there waiting. *What is he waiting for?* As I would get ready to leave my street, I wouldn't see him, then as I turned onto the main road, he would appear. It was really freaking me out since every time I came around the corner, he was facing me and moving in my direction as if he knew I could see him. What was it that he wanted to talk to me about? Even though I preferred not to get involved in messages from spirits to the living, I couldn't seem to avoid it.

The next day, one of the neighbors came by and said, "If you've noticed all the police at the corner house, it's because the guy who lived there committed suicide in his car a week ago." I must have had a zoned-out appearance on my face because the neighbor asked if I was okay. *A week ago*, I thought. *That's exactly when I heard a gunshot and the man started standing on the corner every time I passed by. Oh no, I should walk down there and help him.* I didn't want to do it while the neighbor was outside, so I thought, *I'll wait until tomorrow.*

When I woke up the next morning, I glanced to the wall where there was usually a line of spirits waiting in my bedroom for the moment I'd wake up so they could begin communicating. The spirits changed day to day depending on whose loved ones I would talk to. Those present that morning would have to wait until I went down and saw the man on the corner. The spirits who came could be anyone. For example, some spirits who showed up might be related to a waiter or waitress who would cross paths with me when they brought out my lunch. The deceased knew if a loved one would be talking to me, even if it was a casual encounter while I was out and about.

As I walked to the corner of my street, I felt intense anxiety. The house where the spirit had been standing was within view, and as I approached, he was there. I stayed twenty feet away from the edge of his property. He appeared to feel stressed, and I knew he was glad that I was there to communicate with him. I noticed by the light around his energy field that he had gone into the light and wasn't stuck. *So what does he need to tell me?* I thought.

He said, "I've wanted to talk to you to teach you something you didn't know. My name is Lieutenant Henry Callahan. Some spiritual people say when a person commits suicide, they have to start their whole life all over again." He told me he had served in Desert Storm, and after being injured on his tour, he felt useless. He had one daughter who lived up north and was married. He felt that he could no longer have a normal life and didn't know how to go on. Henry explained that when someone commits suicide, they don't have to redo their whole life, just the part they couldn't accept and decided was their reason for the suicide.

As he was talking about his situation and what happened step-by-step, Archangel Raphael came in, explaining that Henry knew I needed that knowledge to share with others. Archangel Raphael said it was more for people to know and understand that whatever their situation was, they could change it by asking for help while in the human experience. Once they got to the other side, they would need to set up another life that would ultimately lead them back to the same emotions and feelings they'd decided to exit with suicide. Their higher self would set it up so that they could triumph rather than throw in the towel. Henry continued to explain what he'd experienced after he crossed. He would be building up his light body and getting ready to come back into the physical. Henry thanked me for acknowledging him and for coming to see him. He waved and vanished.

Prior to stopping and talking to Henry, I had made an appointment with Belinda Smart. When we began the session, she said there was something different going on in my energy. I explained what had happened with Henry, and she said, "Let's go in while we do the session and clear any sadness associated with that property so you're not feeling it each time you have to drive past." I was delighted with that idea, and as we went in and the portal began to open to clear the energy, we noticed about a thousand souls going through the portal. The souls were all coming from two miles away. Belinda asked, "What is two miles away causing all the souls to come up?" And then it came to me—it was an Alzheimer's facility. She said, "Look at all the souls," as we both watched and wondered how they made it through the portal that we had opened up to clear Henry's house. It was beautiful.

"Belinda," I asked, "what is the reason for this?"

Belinda said it was apparently due to those souls being confused and not knowing to go to the light. They must have been lingering around the facility. She said, "Don't be surprised if you open up a portal for clearing and you see more souls leave from that place from time to time as more people may come there to live and die. Some spirits with those conditions get confused, not knowing to go into the light, so they continue to linger around. When we open a portal like this, it gives them the opportunity to get to the other side."

We continued our session, which was amazing as always, and I thanked her. After I got off the phone, I noticed some unusual things. I could actually hear the birds that were outside in the trees communicating with me. Hearing an animal communicate their thoughts or desires was expected with the two dogs I had, but I didn't often get messages from wildlife. The backyard was fairly large, and there were lots of tall trees. It actually sounded like a bird sanctuary when I stood in the center of the yard. I could hear chirps, I could hear them talking to each other, and I could hear them singing. Now they were asking for me to turn on the water. I actually heard them say, "Turn on the sprinkler." So I put the sprinkler on the end of the hose, carefully situating it so it was in the center of the yard, and turned it on. When I got back inside, they said, "Thank you." My heart felt like it was glowing. Not only could I hear them communicating, but I could also hear the wind and the sun. The sounds the wind and the sun were making were only frequency. I felt like I had stepped into a whole different dimension where everything was completely clear, yet much more inter-dimensional than ever before.

My days were packed at that point. I was not only teaching a spiritual class every other Saturday, but I was also working the practice during the week and taking calls from the psychic network hotline from random callers. There was one particular call I will never forget. The woman said, "Do you need a birthday in order to read a person?"

I said, "No, just the first name and what they go by. No last names, please."

She said her first name. Immediately, I felt a hotel room, then I found a deep passion she felt for a male coworker. I told her, "The first thing that comes up is you on the road living in hotel rooms. I also see a man connected to your heart who is unavailable to you. What is it that you want me to look into?"

She said, "You are very good; someone gave me your name, and they were right about you." She asked me a series of questions, none of which would've made sense to anyone else, but I knew she was testing me. We got off the phone, and I kept working. Two and a half hours later, she called me back. At that point, she was three sheets to the wind and could no longer form sentences. I told her I felt it would be better if she waited and called me back the next day, as I was concerned she wouldn't remember what we talked about. She insisted on staying on the phone and said she was writing everything down, and if I wanted, she could even record it so she could listen to it the next day. I told her that was fine, she could record it, and she began to ask me about the guy who I saw she was so passionate about. She told me she worked with intelligence officers and was a seer like me. I immediately felt sad for her, as I knew that must be a tough job. There was no way I could ever do that—it would be stressful, and I knew whenever someone was in fear mode or anxious, there was no way they could see what they needed to see. I would probably be in fear mode, as I'm sure most of the things they had her look at were tough. We ended the call, but I didn't feel it would be the last time I would hear from her. What was it I needed to know from that call? When something is highlighted that I'm either experiencing or hearing, I know there's something more for me to learn.

***

While working as a professional psychic, I've met some of the most interesting people, and I'm very thankful that the cornerstone of my business has been word-of-mouth. I never advertised, and I really never thought I needed to. I always felt that I would reach the people who I was supposed to read for, and they would get the messages they needed. I knew lots of other intuits and psychics, so when I felt the situation would be better handled by someone else, I would often refer people over. I've read for other psychics, and some of them would even refer clients to me. The energy workers who I've referred people over to have never referred anybody back. When I sat with that, asking why that was the situation with energy workers, I was guided that they were so worried about whether they were going to get clients or not, they didn't want to send any away even if it was something they couldn't help with. That was super profound. They were in the business to do energy work, and healing is supposed to be something we want for everyone. I knew I wasn't ready to read for certain things yet, like some child abuse situations similar to those that I had not quite cleared from my own template and was still working through. I needed to send those individuals to someone else, as I knew they would be better than I could be, given the situation.

A vibration that was starting in my body had been moving up. It was moving slowly, and I could only feel it as I was waking up.

When I asked what it was, I felt it was "the awakening." It wasn't like what people talk about with yoga or the kundalini—it was something different.

A dream that I'd had my whole life began to unfold. I knew I had lived in France in a lifetime right before this one. I had been born to a fifteen-year-old girl who named me Victoria, and my dad was a GI. That short lifetime would end with my murder in 1945. The guy I used to see at the foot of my bed every time something bad happened when I was a child was my father from that lifetime. He never even knew I existed while he was alive but vowed to keep an eye on me until he was ready to reincarnate. My mom in that lifetime was forced to give me up, and that's how I ended up in an orphanage. When the orphanage closed, they took those of us who were able to walk and led us out the back door. I lived in the back alley with a few other orphans. My dress was tattered, and my skin was dirty. My feet were scarred from cuts because I lacked shoes. I even remembered a couple of us older kids taking off the shoes we were outgrowing and giving them to the smaller children who had outgrown theirs.

One of the men on the street who I had seen with his wife killed me. I finally saw the end of that life when his hands were clasped around my throat before I entered the light. I spent some time trying to research orphanages from 1943 to 1945 in France. During the session with Belinda Smart, it was revealed I should just allow it to clear—that was then, and this is now. She explained how part of my need to see the dream was to open it up and help me clear it, and clearing it was helping me to awaken and accept who I was.

***

It was summertime, and our neighbor was throwing a party. The host of the party explained that some of the other neighbors would be arriving late and talked about a cute little family who lived on the corner and how they were coming. As they were walking up, I could see their energy field very clearly. It was 6:30 p.m., and the brightness of the sun was reduced as it was going down. The husband and wife weren't emotionally connected at all. The woman introduced herself as Mrs. Patrick, which was weird because we were an informal group. After they had made their way through the line and greeted everyone, they loaded up their plates and grabbed a seat under the trees. I knew by then that if someone was meant to talk to me or teach me something, they would find me. Mrs. Patrick sat down, then decided to pick up her lawn chair and move it closer to me. As she took a bite of her food, she asked what I did for work. I felt very strongly that she already knew what I did; she just needed an opening line to ask me a question. I told her, "I'm a psychic medium, and my primary focus is the body."

In a very judgmental voice, she said, "That's interesting. So do you believe in God?"

"I do believe in God," I answered, nodding. I could see in her energy field she was suspicious her husband was having an affair. What she didn't know was that he'd had several. I wanted to go because I knew deep down that she was looking for free information, but I had come for a relaxing afternoon. I excused myself, picked up my plate and cup, and walked over to the trash can. I thanked the hostess who invited us and let her know that I had to get home—there were some things I needed to take care of.

As I was walking back, I thought about how many other times I'd been approached in similar situations. There were times when I was out for lunch and the kids were at school when I'd been approached by females who wanted to join me. I knew it happened because there was either something they needed to learn or something I needed to learn. When I went to bed that night, I gave careful consideration and asked God why I ran across those types of people on my path. The frequency came back and said, "Sometimes it happens so that blockages that have kept them from finding themselves can begin to open due to the light you activate within them."

"How does a light activate?" I asked.

"It has to do with the energies of the starseeds from previous lifetimes or the incarnation of their true soul origin being awakened." Starseeds are advanced spiritual beings, typically from other planets or realms. They are considered to be old souls that sometimes incarnate back to Earth in an effort to help bring positive light to humanity.

"Okay, so the lady who sat next to me at the neighborhood party—did she experience such activation, I hope?"

"Yes, it's going to help her understand the truth that her suspicions are valid and that she can find the strength to be able to move forward and have the life and love that she wants." The frequency came in again and said, "Sometimes it's about them releasing judgment they have felt against themselves, and the opportunity to release it comes by not judging you."

When I woke up in the morning, my right foot was over my left foot, and my arms were out to my sides as I was lying in the center of my bed on my back. I was having a hard time opening my eyes while still in that position. I lay there, peeking at the ceiling. "God," I said out loud, "what's going on? Why did I wake up like this?" When I was finally able to emerge from the bed, I loaded the toothpaste on my toothbrush and looked in the mirror as I was brushing my teeth. Trying to find every human explanation for why I woke up that way, the first was, *Am I about to go through baptism by fire? No, it can't be that.* I felt like I'd gone through baptism by fire when I was a child, when I was a teen, and when I was an adult. I ended up taking notes on how I'd felt when I woke up and thought I would wait and revisit it later.

Chapter Nine

The Major

The week was going fine for a typical Tuesday. There had been no extra stressors whatsoever, the kids were happy, and prosperity was flowing in. That night, I was comfy and cozy, with clean sheets on my bed. I knew that as soon as I closed my eyes, I was going to sleep great. In fact, I could barely even keep my eyes open as I crawled into bed. I fell asleep immediately. My spirit guides gathered around me and guided me to the other side as I went through a dimension. As I did, I became very cold—not just chilly, but cold to the bone. I was shivering as I made my way through the dimension. When I reached the far point of my path, they had me lay down. My father from this lifetime came to me and said, "Mary, I'm so glad you are here. So you finished your mission?"

Before I could even register what he was saying, one of my guides told him, "No, we brought her here so she could visit and see what it's like when she's teaching others." I was still shivering, and the guides laid something over me that was not a real blanket even though it looked like one. It was a sheet of light that was placed over my body from the neck down. Then they began to work on me. At that point,

I was completely out. Before my father greeted me, I remember that I was really scared and frightened because I knew where they were taking me and what they were going to show me, yet I don't remember anything after that. I must have been knocked out.

When I woke up, I sat up in bed, trying to remind myself that I was still alive. I touched the bed with my palms to make sure it was solid, unlike the dimension I'd just visited. I got up and allowed my feet to glide across the floor in the mindset to anchor myself. I walked down the hallway and looked into Breezy and Zach's room. They were sleeping. *They're here. I'm not dead*, I thought. I walked to the window to look out at the night sky, then I walked back to the bed. I assured myself again that I was still alive and very much in the physical.

The next morning, I called Belinda Smart. I explained to her exactly what happened the night before, and she said, "Oh, Katharine, you got to experience something amazing. You experienced the death process without having to go through it. You're very lucky. Many people have to experience near-death through a trauma or connected to an accident. You can now understand and teach others about it." Our session mostly consisted of removing the fear that I had stepped into while in the other dimension—a fear that seemed to belong to others besides me. It was something Belinda explained that would help my clients.

"The cold feeling of that night was unexplainable," I told her.

Belinda said, "It was only cold because you weren't ready to stay, and your Earth connection had a temperature difference that is not normally an issue."

That weird cold-to-the-bone feeling lingered with me all day. It was not the cold part that I was surprised about, but the very *aware* feeling of the depth of my bones. Feeling that meant one thing: it was the removal of old programs put in place by the crooked and greedy ways of humanity. My spirit guides explained it as the removal of lifetimes where I may have been involved in or experienced with humanity so I could help empower others with a brand new template in this life.

The next night, I sat with my spirit guides and asked, "Why did my dad seem so happy to see me? And why did he think I was actually dead?"

The guides told me that deceased loved ones don't know our life plan. They may know some of the experiences that we plan to have, but they don't know our blueprints; only our spirit guides, angels, our higher self, and God know our blueprints. As my mind wrapped around that, I realized he simply saw me there and thought it was good to see me. Then once he realized I was just visiting, he knew he would see me again when I was ready or when I would visit.

The next day was going great and flying by; I felt like I was in the zone with work. Things felt so easy in the readings that I was doing. It felt as if something had changed within me after the experience of death. Before a question was even asked, I would hear the answer to it. As I was getting finished with what I thought was my last call for the day, the phone rang. It was a man with a deep voice I'd never read for. He introduced himself as Austin Hart and said he would like me to take a look into a legal situation he was dealing with. He proceeded to ask me a few questions, and I answered them. I had a peculiar feeling like nothing I'd experienced in my spirit before. It was not a physical sensation; it was a frequency sensation. *Okay, now this is weird*, I thought.

It wasn't a bad sensation, just different and unexplainable. I felt in some way he might make me face my truths and perhaps something that I wasn't ready to deal with, so I thought I would block his number to avoid reading for him again. When I came back from lunch, I finished my work and didn't think about Austin again.

The following week as I was going about my day, the phone rang, and it was Austin. That time I felt an even more intense frequency. *Oh no*, I thought. *Why didn't I block him? How could I have forgotten?* I realized I'd have to read for him since he was already on the phone with me. He asked a few questions, and I answered. When I looked into his energy field, I saw blue—the same color blue that I had around my energy field. He wasn't the only person I'd seen with blue in their energy field before. There's one specific shade of blue that indicates if someone flew through a particular grid when they incarnated. That really didn't mean anything; there were lots of "blue ray" people that I wasn't attracted to. But I felt a different energy with Austin. There was something about his voice that drew me in, and I was beginning to feel hooked. When we got off the phone, he sent me an email with his photo attached. He was wearing his military dress blues uniform and was just all-around dreamy. I never cared what clients looked like and never felt drawn in by their voice frequency before. A few weeks went by, and I couldn't shake the feeling I'd experienced when talking to Austin.

He called a few more times before the conversation turned personal. He explained that he had lost his son, Alex, only a year and a half prior, then his life fell apart. He said when he decided to call a psychic about his situation, my photo kept coming up on his computer, but he blew it off, thinking I wouldn't know much since I appeared pretty and he was looking for someone who seemed more seasoned. My photo continued to come up in a few more searches, so he began to feel like it was his son who led him to me. We spent a while talking on the phone, and when I got off, I thought, *What have I done?* I'd never crossed the line of feeling attracted to a client. Then I thought, *I shouldn't worry too much about it because he lives several states away.*

A couple of months went by, and things were changing with Austin's case. We were also talking just about every day. It felt super strange. I was talking to at least a hundred clients a week, yet this one had a frequency that pulled me in. *Wait a minute*, I thought. *When people are supposed to experience something karmic, there's something that draws them in.* I prayed, "Please, God, don't let this be karmic."

Austin had served twenty years in the US Army; he had never had any previous issues with the law, and yet the state DA was looking for blood. An alleged "victim" said that Austin attacked him in his home. I knew Austin didn't attack him, so why was the alleged victim upset? Well, Austin was dating his ex-wife. Austin shouldn't have gone over there to tell him off, but he did, and it left it open for the man to say whatever he wanted. What Austin didn't know was when someone told me a story, regardless of whether it was true or false, I saw exactly what had happened. I knew he was telling the truth.

Time seemed to be flying by, and when the court date came up, he was charged with a serious felony. Austin took a polygraph test and passed, so with the advice of his lawyer, he pled "guilty by convenience." The lawyer believed the judge would see the truth of the case and only give him probation, but when sentencing day came, the judge made the surprising choice to give him seven years. Austin had begun to lose hope, as he felt his country turned its back on him to take the word of a man who already had a criminal history. The cautionary tale is if someone makes you upset, don't go to their house because they can say anything happened.

I was really baffled as to why the whole situation was happening. I knew that for whatever reason, there were still things he needed to learn and things he needed to see. I had set an appointment with Belinda so I could update her. After the call, I felt better. We both agreed that whatever needed to happen would eventually work out for the reasons God intended. It's important for me to note that Austin served his country, was an avid volunteer, and was the kind of guy who never met anyone who hadn't liked him until then.

I still felt emotionally connected to him, but I had to keep going. Work was incredibly busy, and being a mom was my real job in itself. I'd had the majority of my clients since day one of starting my practice, though I would periodically get a new wave of people all dealing with similar issues. One week in particular was really crazy. I had several women contact me who were either trying to leave a religion or their cultural beliefs. In many situations, it entangled both of those categories. I had six new clients who were all of the Muslim faith trying to leave their marriages due to abuse they'd been experiencing. Then I had two people from the Church of Jesus Christ of Latter-day Saints trying to make plans to escape an even worse nightmare. I knew whenever God showed me things from the past, it was so that I could understand the underlying issues in current situations.

I have said it before and will say it again—when the universe wants us to learn something, it will show us until we master the information.

I was still struggling to understand the meaning of my strong feelings for Austin. I knew my natural love for people and animals was boundless. Even some of my closest friends were amazed at how my emotions were so open to deeply love humans and animals. I chose to only see the good in them. But with Austin, my feelings went beyond the warmth I usually experience toward people.

Austin called and wanted to talk about his house. It was too late to list it for sale, and he just wanted to let it go into foreclosure. All of Austin's beliefs in the law and justice system were shattered with the heavy blow of his unjust sentence. He wanted to die. We spent four hours on the phone as I told him he would get through it and I would help him. He said he missed his son and wanted to see him again. It was a difficult conversation, as I had to explain that no one escapes life's lessons—not even through death. I told him perhaps I was too close to him to get a proper read on the lessons he most needed to learn. When people are connected, they may have a spiritual contract, and personal insights about each other would not be shown until the spiritual contract is worked out. This is true for one's own offspring. The contract can be too emotionally intertwined; it can be difficult to look past a desired outcome. Everyone, even those who are awakening, are on a journey of learning. Even if it's not the same lesson as ours, the lesson for a loved one may be hidden until the right combination of spiritual growth and understanding is in place.

He told me that everything he had been living for was ripped out from under him. And with his son gone, there was nothing left. I told him he needed to see things through in this life, as I knew from prior readings on suicide that whatever one thinks is too tough to endure, those are the things that will be obstacles in the next life that they will still have to overcome. He asked if I would be willing to handle his bankruptcy and to have a power of attorney so when he was serving his sentence, I could send him money from his account. I agreed but still felt strange. Here was a man I'd never met in person, yet I was handling his personal affairs and his bankruptcy and coordinating the shipping of all his belongings.

Please, God. Please show me what I'm supposed to do, I prayed. That night, after I fell asleep, I felt a vibration in my legs in the inner core of my nervous system. It felt like the vibration was trying to move, but it was blocked. Despite the energy I could feel pushing up, I was staying in the same place. When I finally opened my eyes, I was lying on my right side. I saw a spirit near the wall and recognized that his frequency identified as Alex, Austin's son. Alex was standing there looking at me as if he were waiting patiently for me to acknowledge him. When I fully opened my eyes, he seemed happy. I affirmed that I knew who he was as I made my way past him and walked to the restroom. When I returned, he told me that he would be there for his dad and that the lesson his father needed to learn was trust. *Trust? What does that even mean?*

During that visit from Alex, I noticed him coming in from the left side, whereas normally, deceased people come in from the right-side portal. He told me that it was because he lived at the Galactic Center, so that's the portal he needed to come through for visits. The phone was ringing down the hall, so I made my way to the office with Alex following. Austin was on the phone. "I know this is crazy, but I saw a lady on YouTube who does twin flame readings," he said.

I knew nothing about twin flames—it wasn't a topic I paid any attention to.

Previously, I had thought it wasn't significant enough to warrant putting any of my energy toward it. I knew that when people would use the term "soulmates," they often misunderstood what it meant. People have many soulmates because soulmates are from their soul family. A soul family is a group of souls who usually incarnate around the same time so they can experience lifetimes together. Some members of the soul family will stay on the other side as the rest have their human experiences. When contracts are fulfilled and they have learned what was needed while balancing karma, then a soul no longer has to incarnate.

Austin told me he'd met with the woman from YouTube, and when he asked about me, she said, "Yes, you guys are absolutely twin flames." I wasn't completely sold even though I was attracted to him. Did I want to sleep with him? Yes. Did I want to be with him? Yes. The problem was I had never felt anybody could truly love me. Yet he was happy, and I wanted to see him happy. I wanted him to see he had something to live for, and it felt great. I never considered whether the twin flame reader told everyone that they were with their twin flame or were going to be with their twin. Did she ever tell someone that they were not?

While my own practice was going great, I was still taking calls on the psychic hotline. People would primarily call for love readings. Love questions were easy to read since all I would need to do was tune in to their spirit guides, angels, and their higher self. I would listen to what they would say and parrot it back to the client. If the spirit guide told me that the relationship in question was not going to last, I would relay that message. When someone would call about twin flames, I felt creeped out about doing the reading because I didn't want to give the people false hope when I didn't see myself as a twin flame reader. In fact, I would think, *Who the hell is a twin flame reader—if it's really even a thing*? I would tell the client what their spirit guide was saying about their love interest. When someone would ask if it was their twin flame, their spirit guides would often look at me as if they knew I knew the answer. I would explain to the client that I looked for soul contracts and then checked to see if they were karmic. If there was no soul contract, it meant they didn't have anything of substance with that person, much less a long-term relationship opportunity together. I would often refer those clients to people who promoted themselves as twin flame readers.

I had received several calls where I didn't believe the person in question was connected to the caller, whether it was someone they cared for or just a one-night stand. There was one girl named Crystal who had been institutionalized by her mother with the support of her doctors. Crystal told me she believed that Colin Farrell was her twin flame. I didn't negate anything she said; I just went in with her spirit guides to ask if she was spiritually connected to him in any way. I heard "no," and I was told that she often believed that male celebrities were connected to her and that they gave her messages through interviews. She asked me if I knew anybody who was a twin flame reader and mentioned that she had seen some on YouTube. I told her about the one Austin found. She was really great with energy work, but I still wasn't sold on her twin flame belief. I wanted to believe that there was love. I wanted to believe that there was another half waiting for people. Deep down, I couldn't decipher what was keeping me from believing in twin flames. I couldn't tell if it was just my jaded experiences or if it was divine knowledge.

Crystal eagerly asked for the name of the twin flame reader so she could call her for a session.

I knew that if the twin flame reader were genuine about seeing people's twin flames, she would tell Crystal that Colin Farrell was not her twin. A few weeks later, Crystal called. She was so excited. She had happiness in her voice, and she said the twin flame reader told her that Colin was indeed her twin flame and that they would be together. I immediately felt that was completely wrong. *Why would this twin flame reader do that? This girl is very unstable, and it was wrong to get her hopes up.* From looking at her and looking at Colin Farrell's energy, I knew that there was no energy match there. That meant they had no paths destined to join. I even looked to see if there were any contracts the two of them had together in past lives, and there were absolutely none. Crystal told me that the twin flame reader even told her to take a trip back East and that by going there, it would help open up her ability to be with him. However, I knew something the twin flame reader didn't know. Crystal wasn't allowed to travel anywhere outside of her home for more than five or ten minutes unless she was accompanied by her mother.

I wanted to think the best about the twin flame reader and thought maybe Crystal didn't say Colin Farrell—maybe she said Colin. So I looked into Crystal's energy to see if there was anyone on her path named Colin. Again, there was nobody in her path with the name of Colin that she was to meet up with in this life. I really wanted to believe that this twin flame person didn't mislead all those people just to make them feel good or to keep selling sessions. But it didn't look good. There were even meditations she said would help them to attract their twin flame.

Later that week, I was reading for a client named Mohammed. At the time, I had been reading for him for nine years. He was a doctor who had a no-nonsense attitude when it came to medicine, but he had a great sense of humor. When he and I had a session, it was usually about his practice and things I saw in his patients that he might be missing. I had several clients who were in the medical field that I would read for in similar ways. It seems that malpractice had gotten so expensive that if there were any issues whatsoever, the doctor would go in front of the board about things that could have been avoided. His mother had set him up with his wife through a matchmaker, and while he felt like getting married was the right thing at the time, it never felt like he was in love the way he imagined love to be, and the passion had never been there.

Periodically, he would ask me what kinds of readings I would do for other clients. I explained that I got lots of questions about love, life, and death. "So how do you answer love questions?" he asked. I explained that when a client was interested in a particular person, I had them say their first name and the other person's first name or the nickname they went by, and as they did, I followed the frequency looking for the match. If there was no match, I'd know there was no long-term future between those people. I also looked for spiritual contracts. If there was one, I'd check if it was a karmic contract—which usually meant it would end in tears—or if what they had was just a spiritual contract for an experience. I then explained the meaning of "twin flames" and told him it had been a hot word lately. Furthermore, I explained that many twin flame readers promised that they could deliver one's counterpart if the person adhered to doing certain things to draw in their twin flame. After explaining that, he wanted me to tell him where he could find a person who advertised expertise in twin flame connections. I gave him the name of the same one I gave to Crystal. I told him she had several videos on YouTube and told people there were meditations and sessions that activated starseeds to help draw in their twin flame. She also said she could remove blockages that kept twin flames from one another. I could tell there was a part of him that was very interested in the whole process from a scientific standpoint. I told him her energy work was amazing, but the whole twin flame thing never felt right to me. I'd read for people I saw identical matches for and told those clients that the person in question was the one I saw them marrying. If there was no match in the energy field, it didn't matter what the person did. They could be with the hottest person they'd ever encountered, yet the relationship would go nowhere if it wasn't contracted. I could see I had piqued his interest with the twin flame conversation, and he asked for the woman's contact information. He set up an appointment with her later that day.

The following morning, I had lots to do. I needed to go to the bank and get a cashier's check for nine thousand dollars so I could send it to the bankruptcy attorney for Austin's filing. I never had trouble spending money, even when I'd written a check out for a car that I'd purchased. Large numbers on paper never bothered me until I had to write a check out for Austin's bankruptcy. My hand was shaking the whole time I wrote that check. It's hard feeling like you're spending someone else's money, even when it's for them. It really stressed me out.

I made it a lighter workday, considering there were other things I needed to do. I was feeling completely fatigued. The worry for Austin and everything else going on left me drained. I could feel the energy of bitterness. I didn't feel like it was toward Austin, the kids, or work; it just seemed like a general feeling—as if I were picking something up from the collective consciousness. I've noticed that when big things are about to happen in the world, whether it's sad or happy, my psychic antenna tends to pick up the collective consciousness as a whole. My anxiety got so bad that at that point in my life, driving had become such a difficult task I had to get Breezy to drive me places. I couldn't stay focused in the here-and-now dimension, especially while driving. The spirits who lined the freeways and roadways from car accidents who didn't know they had passed were such distractions for me. Not only did I see spirits waiting alongside the road, but I would also see exactly what had happened when I merely looked at them and wondered why they were there.

I contacted the twin flame reader, who I'd had energy work from before, and she was able to squeeze me in. The energy work was amazing. I really felt a shift and a true clearing. I was really grateful, and I felt I could proceed with the day. Later that evening, I got a text from Mohammed. He said if I was awake, he'd like to talk, and he would make it quick. Mohammed was one of my VIP clients, which meant he could do more than just set up sessions; he had access to be able to text me even for quick questions. As soon as I answered the text, my phone rang. He told me he had a session with the twin flame reader. He told her he was married and wanted to know if his wife was his twin flame and that he'd been thinking about a woman named Naya that he was in residency with. He told me the twin flame reader told him, "Yes, Naya is your twin, and you will reconnect at a medical convention. She will instantly change her life to be with you." She also went on to say that he would need to divorce his current wife in order to be with Naya because Naya was not the type of woman to be open to waiting for a divorce.

As he told me this, I could sense it was a trap for the twin flame reader. "So, what's the scoop?" I asked with a laugh. He went on to explain that Naya was indeed a person he was in residency with, but she was a lesbian and had been in a committed partnership the whole time he had known her. He then said, "I wanted to share my experience in the session because while she is good at doing energy work, she has no idea about twin flames. I didn't acknowledge to her that there was nothing between Naya and me. The twin flame reader even went on to say that we would be together and that we would be happy as a couple."

After the call with Mohammed, I lay there thinking about Austin. He was so hopeful about the twin flame magic he thought he and I shared. I didn't want to share with him what I knew about Crystal and Mohammad's experience with the reader.

After my energy work with the twin flame reader, I signed up to participate in one of her online Saturday morning classes. It was rather sad how different people would ask questions and I would hear the answer immediately. I never said anything. I let the twin flame reader answer as she would—after all, she was the one in charge of the class. One of the ladies in the class had mentioned that she was getting these sensations in her chest, and the twin flame reader told her that it was the high heart opening for her twin flame. I immediately knew that was wrong. The online platform we were using allowed a chat option where participants could type a message to others in the meeting. I immediately opened the chat box and sent the twin flame reader a message saying that the woman asking the question about the sensation in her chest needed to go and be looked at by a doctor because she hadn't had a regular physical exam in over twenty years. The last time she'd gone to a doctor for a full exam was after she had her baby. I noticed the twin flame reader's eyes right at the moment when she read the message. Her eyes got very wide because the woman who had asked the question was in her sixties. Again, I sent a message saying that the woman in her sixties needs to go and tell her doctor. At that moment, the twin flame reader asked the woman, "When was the last time you went to a doctor and had a full exam?" The woman, who was still touching her heart, responded that she hadn't been for a full exam since she had her baby. Again, the reader's eyes grew wider with awe because she still didn't know what I did for a living. She was surprised that I knew what I had told her. I think it's because I never told people what I did, and she just thought I was one of the people desperate for her advice and desperate to find love. At the end of the day, I really couldn't give less of a shit about finding love because I'd already resigned myself to believe that no one would truly love me aside from Breezy and Zach.

***

My relationship with Mom seemed to be getting better. One day while she was attending her Red Hat Society meeting, she was talking to a woman named Nancy about health issues she was healing from. Nancy went on to say the woman who helped her was a psychic. She said the psychic just knew things and had really helped her with some of her physical ailments. Mom was intrigued. "What's her name? Is she local?" Mom asked her.

Nancy answered, happy to share the information. "She's local; she lives in The Woodlands."

Mom had no idea Nancy was talking about me. Nancy said, "Here's her card; you can have it. I have all of her contact information in my phone."

Mom glanced down and saw my face. "That's my daughter," she said with a laugh.

"Oh, then you definitely don't need the card. You must be so proud—your daughter is amazing. I actually found your Katharine through one of my neighbors who had a reading with her." Nancy went on to brag about the session, saying she'd never met anyone able to see so much and that she'd had readings with several psychics in the past that were very vague.

When Mom would mention other psychics to me, I would get mad because I knew there wasn't much to their gifts, and for years she shrugged my gifts off and made me feel bad for the things I knew. She only became open to psychics in her older years when they became more widely covered in the media.

Chapter Ten

The Knowing

In 2019, I could tell that the relationship between Mom and I was in a better place than it had ever been before. The only troubling thing was that every time she called me, she wanted to ask me psychic questions. It was frustrating because it's what I spent my days doing for work. I was reading from sunup to sundown.

I wanted our visits to be fun so we could have the mother-daughter relationship I'd wanted with her for years. Even when she came over to visit me, she would want to talk to a deceased relative. On many occasions, I would read for her and ask questions of any relative she wanted. My mom would usually want to know how Dad was doing on the other side. When I would see him, I would see him hiking outside. The first time I called him forward, I noticed that he had two dogs with him. "Dad, who are the two dogs with you?" I asked. He told me one was the stray dog that he had shot many decades prior when it was barking with our dog Honey in the night, and the other was one my mom had asked him to take and drop off somewhere. He explained that caring for the dogs was part of the spiritual learning that he needed to help elevate his soul. He explained that when an animal comes to someone, regardless of the circumstance, they are there to help elevate the person's soul and help elevate their heart. Suddenly, so much more knowledge than what he was speaking at that moment was being downloaded into my body. It felt as if my mind and body were a computer.

Mom was always so grateful after the communications with Dad. She would also mention how much she loved him.

On one particular evening, she asked me to call forward her sister who had passed. As my aunt came forward, she appeared so happy to see us together and began to tell us about what she did in heaven. She explained that she had a job there where she helped line up souls with their other family members so they could reincarnate together and their contracts and karma could be balanced. I asked her to explain a little bit more by comparing her job to an occupation that we could understand on Earth. My aunt said the closest thing would be a recruiting center. She recruited others for positions and helped each individual find the perfect opportunity to have when they incarnated so they could balance as much as possible with the time they were given. Mom and I were so fascinated by the information she was teaching us.

Then Mom asked a question that I intuitively knew the answer to but was shocked to hear her ask. Mom asked why she always slept with my grandmother as a child and never saw her mom and dad share a room. My aunt looked at me, knowing that my mom knew the answer but had pushed it down in the depths of her human memory so she wouldn't feel ashamed. My aunt placed both hands over the light that was emitting from her heart. She explained that their father had molested all of the girls in their family, and they all chose to marry young so they could get out of the house as quickly as they could. There was such a large age gap between my mother and her sisters that they had already gotten married when she was born, so she was the only one left at home. My grandmother would have her sleep with her in order to protect her in hopes that she wouldn't have to go through what her sisters did. As I was relaying this to Mom word for word from my aunt, Mom looked directly at me as if she was shocked that I was communicating the information. She knew it was true, and I could see the fear in her energy as her field filled with dark orange that was shattered by shame and guilt. The shame and guilt were from a lifelong belief that she had done something wrong when really she hadn't. She had carried the belief since childhood but hadn't tapped in to find out why. Her father had made his choices, and he had karma that he would eventually have to balance.

At that moment, everything about how she treated me as a child and a young teen made sense to me. She had taken a shame that she had pushed down and projected it onto me. That must've been the emotion that was tied to her internally every time she got mad at me for talking to my dad or any time he showed me any small amount of affection by patting my head. It all made so much sense: burning my mouth with peppers, the happy feeling she had when she got Dad to whip us with a belt, and all the times she just didn't want me home. At that moment, all the feelings I had for so many years when I felt like a victim and all of the feelings I had from knowing I had a mom who didn't love me completely vanished. I realized I was sitting at a new vantage point by being able to see all the emotions I'd ever felt as if I were on the right hand of God, watching this movie unfold. Mom tried to brush off what my aunt said, adding, "This all makes sense, but I remember none of it, and I never knew why I always slept with my mother."

***

HOW I FOUND MY SUPERPOWERS

Work was extremely busy, and I was feeling a lot of pressure. Some of the clients I had at that point were people you just didn't want to mess up with. I had to be on my game at all times. I couldn't miss a beat when I was looking into any situation they would call me for. I was not only reading for several people in the medical community, but I was also reading for several cases of suicide and abuse. With the readings that I did, I got the information from my clients' spirit guides or from a deceased person themself so I could witness what had happened to them. The knowledge of why it happened came to me shortly after watching.

I was teaching psychic development classes every other Saturday. I had some of the most amazing people come to those classes, some of whom had traveled all over the world seeking spiritual guidance. One particular couple who came in changed my perspective about language. As the couple traveled the world, they would look for the most spiritually guided people they could find so they could have healing sessions and psychic readings with them. I'm not quite sure how they got my name. Perhaps I will ask the wife, Sabrina, one day, but I'll never forget the first time she and her husband, Marsh, came to a healing class. I asked for a volunteer to lie on the table so I could demonstrate hand placement for healing. Marsh happily volunteered and proceeded to lie down on the table. Everyone gathered around as I explained that we were going to allow him to close his eyes for a moment. As I began to go in and ask his angels, his spirit guides, and his deceased loved ones to come for the healing, I noticed a male spirit step to my right side who began talking to me in Japanese. The funny thing is, I don't speak Japanese, but I understood every word he said. I translated everything word for word to Sabrina. During that process, Marsh was completely knocked out. I told her there was a very handsome Japanese man standing there. The man told me that he loved Marsh and that Marsh was one of his students during his lifetime here. He told me they had a long history together and that Marsh was with him when he decided to cross over to the other side and walk out of his body, making his ascension. While chills ran up my body, I knew I was not the only one experiencing the enlightenment that was happening. I had tears running down my face as I finished relaying the message. I finished up the healing work as I was guided by the spiritual master next to me.

As Marsh came to, Sabrina was so happy she actually had the experience that she'd been wanting. She held Marsh's hand and told him the name of the master who came forward. Marsh was extremely grateful. I couldn't shake the astonishment I had about the way I was able to understand Japanese at that very moment. Why was I able to do it? The frequency came in and explained that on the other side, regardless of the language, the frequency will always translate. That information was mind-blowing. I had believed it was so important for my children to learn every language that they could. We all had our favorite languages we like to learn.

It had been two weeks since the day Marsh's teacher had spoken Japanese to me during the class. Sabrina and Marsh came for another class, and that time they brought a very special robe. It was a silk robe with a beautiful bordered crest, and it tied around at the waist. Marsh explained that since he never had children, no one would ever understand what his spiritual master had meant to him, and because his spiritual master came through during that healing session with me, he wanted me to have the robe. I was very grateful, although I didn't feel deserving of such an honor. I hung the robe up and planned to pray about it later.

Later that day, after class was over, I heard a certain prayer frequency, and the spiritual master came. He told me he wanted me to put on the robe and use it whenever I performed spiritual ceremonies, including weddings and classes. I put the robe on and stood by the window, looking out at the sky. He pointed to a few bushes along the fence and said they were his favorite in his garden. I smiled because the bushes were called 'White by the Gate' camellias, and they bloomed giant white flowers the size of a person's palm. I had just received the bushes a week before when my daughter went to the garden center to find something to put along the gate. I was beginning to think back on all the times when one thing after another began to make sense, and the puzzle pieces were coming together effortlessly.

***

Mom was one of four girls, and one had already crossed to the other side, so I had two aunts left, Auntie Truly and Auntie Frances. Truly was showing signs of memory loss, while Frances seemed just fine. Auntie Frances would call Mom and tell her how worried she was about Truly. Mom was worried and asked what she needed to know for Truly. I heard the frequency say that Frances would be leaving before the end of the year. Then Mom, thinking I was confused, said, "No, Frances is fine; it's Truly who has her medication sitting on the floor."

"I heard you correctly, but God is telling me Frances will be leaving before the end of the year," I told her. It wouldn't have done any good for me to warn Auntie Frances's son or anybody who was close to her, so I didn't mention it to anyone else. Frances actually thought I was crazy and continuously urged Mom to get me some help.

Mom called to update me on her week and explained things she was doing. She told me my stepdad's mother was coming to live with them. She explained that she was upset about it and didn't want her living there. I told her that it was the right thing to do, and if she had the opportunity to have one more week with her mom, she would do it. She was beginning to understand how spirituality worked and that when things happen, it's always for a reason, so she asked, "What's the lesson in her coming to live here?" I hadn't asked that myself but was curious as well. The frequency came across and explained that it was for Mom to learn unconditional love. I got it. I thought back on times in my life when I was homeless, and there was no way that she would've ever let me live with her.

"I do love. I love other people; I love animals; I love my husband," she retorted.

"Mom, loving unconditionally is different. It means loving without conditions and seeing that soul for who they are regardless of their behavior," I told her. Over the next few months, it was not just my mom and my stepdad coming by frequently, it was also my stepdad's mother, and I absolutely loved visiting with her. She was a delight, and when we would go to lunch, I could always get her to eat even when they couldn't.

One day Mom called me and said, "Auntie Frances just passed suddenly, like you said. I thought she was in good physical condition but came to find out she hadn't seen a doctor and she was diabetic. Her organs shut down." Mom explained that she wanted to come out to my side of town and get a new passport since hers had expired, and she wanted me to drive her. My stepdad was completely against getting the passports and told her he didn't understand why they needed them. Mom was frustrated and determined. She told me she absolutely needed her passport for a trip she wanted to take. It was so important to her that she negated every reason why my stepdad didn't want them. "You do understand why the passports are important, right?" she asked. As I heard her say that, I also heard God tell me that she would never need the passport she had just paid for. I sat silently for too long, which is something I typically did when I got frequencies or messages. Mom became even more frustrated, believing my silence meant I was siding with my stepdad. She said, "You never go anywhere anyway—you never want to take a vacation. Passports aren't important to you." I knew she was only aiming her anger toward me. It wasn't that a vacation wasn't important to me; it was that I didn't feel like I could afford one. I felt like I was barely keeping my head above water being a single mom, and if I didn't work, we didn't have money. I didn't get child support for my son; it was always just me. She never could've imagined the type of life I'd had, relying on just myself as the only resource for the family.

Later that night, she called me and said her mother-in-law had slipped and fallen and was taken to the hospital. She asked me if she would be coming back home. As I sat there and looked at the situation, I saw that the hospital would make plans for her to come home, but it wouldn't happen. She was going to pass before coming home.

"Oh no, that's horrible," she said.

Then I heard God's frequency say, "Her mother-in-law was her last contract to learn unconditional love, and instead of accepting her, she refused to learn."

Mom then said, "You know, when it's election time, there's always something major that happens. Well, the election's coming in 2020. What have you seen in readings for that year?"

Suddenly, I had a vision and saw hundreds of thousands of people crossing over to the other side nearly all at once in large pockets all over the world. It was more than I had seen in recent years. "Mom, I see thousands of people leaving in large pockets all over the world during a short period of time," I told her.

"Oh no, am I going to be okay?" she asked.

The frequency came in again and told me, "She will have crossed over by then." I got scared for a moment, and of course, I went silent. Whenever that would happen, whoever I was talking to, whether it was in person or on the phone, always seemed to think I was zoning out on them. They never understood I was getting messages at that exact moment. I'm sure I appeared slow at times—as if I wasn't grasping what the person was telling me—when all along I was actually not only hearing them, but I was also hearing the answer about what was happening. I was scared, and my heart was beating fast as I was worried she would ask me again. *What do I do? What do I say?* My mind was going a million miles a minute. With tears in my eyes, I said, "I want to thank you for all the good times and the bad times, for everything you've taught me, and for being the vehicle to get me here on Earth. You helped me learn everything I needed to know in the way I needed to learn it so I could help other people."

She answered, "Thank you for being my daughter and for teaching me about the spirit world. You've helped me so much, especially in helping me understand how the spirits work on the other side and how they work here to help us." My eyes were overflowing with tears. Thankfully we were on the phone, and she couldn't see me.

Throughout the next week, I wasn't even sure what was happening to me. It was as if God had pulled the information about my mom's impending passing from my memory. It wasn't something I thought about after receiving it. The days were busy, and after a crazy week, I got a call from Mom on Friday morning. "It's Good Friday. Are the kids out of school?" she asked.

"Yes, they're home."

"I'd love to come out! I really want to see you," she said.

I agreed without missing a beat. My whole day had a packed schedule, but I texted and emailed every one of my clients I had booked to reschedule them. When Mom and my stepdad got to my house, we went to breakfast. As we were eating, I could feel myself peering into another dimension around her, and I heard her guide say, "Look at what she's eating. Remember this." I knew that when spirits had told me things like that in the past, it was because there was a crucial lesson coming up so I could help someone else.

We left breakfast and went to run errands together. It was actually an amazing day—one of the best days I'd had with her in a long time. The worry of getting back to clients or getting back home was not on my mind at all. We stopped and went shopping; we stopped for a snack. When we finally got home, we sat in the living room and talked. I felt a heart energy open up within me. I felt like something was being cleared or activated, or maybe even both. I was wrapped up in the emotion. My love for her overwhelmed me as I thought about all the time she hated me and how, in the previous few years, she had become my biggest fan. My heart was clearing. I could feel a lot of energy coming in from God's light. She and my stepdad were ready to leave, so I went upstairs to tell Zach to come down and say goodbye because I knew it would be the last time he would see her in physical form. He was busy playing video games. I walked them out to the car, and as I did, she turned to me and said, "I want to visit with you more often." I hugged her, and as I did, she said, "I need to see you more."

Later that night, at about three o'clock in the morning, there was a banging on the door. I ran downstairs, and it was my stepdad. Crying and frantic, he said, "The ambulance took your mother to the hospital over here. You need to come with me!"

I was just in my nightclothes, so I asked him to sit in the den because I needed to go upstairs and get dressed. I went up to the bedroom, and Mom was there in spirit form. "There's no need for you to go right now; I already crossed to the other side while I was at home."

"Then why did they take you to a hospital?" I asked.

She said they had her heart pumping and that her body was on life-support, waiting for the doctor to come in. She said once the doctor came in, the family would be notified that it would be best to take her off of life support. Mom reiterated, "You don't need to go to the hospital now; just wait."

I went back downstairs to my stepdad and told him I'd have to wait until the morning. He was very frustrated about it. "I'm not going to wait—I can't believe you're not going to see your mother," he said, then he left. I went back upstairs and sat on the bed. I don't remember anything after that; I just fell over asleep. When I woke up, it was six o'clock in the morning, and there was another banging at the door. It was my stepdad again, and he was in tears. I reached out and held him as he explained that the doctor told him the family needed to come say goodbye because she was being held on life support. I called my brother and sister and told them the location of the hospital so I could meet them there.

When we arrived, my stepbrother was there, and I sat and spoke with him for a moment while my stepfather went upstairs with my biological brother and sister to say their goodbyes. However, Mom was in spirit, and she was with me in the lobby. I turned to her. "Don't you think you should go upstairs since they are up there saying goodbye to you? I can see you when this is over."

She said, "Okay," and then she was gone. I sat and talked to my stepbrother for a little bit, then he went upstairs, and I went home. I never did go up to the room. When a loved one passes, we all have to say goodbye in our own way. For my family members, it was in the room before removing the life support. For me, that wasn't necessary—I knew I'd be talking to her later.

The next day I got a call from my stepdad. He said he wanted to hurry up and get all of her personal belongings out of the house now that she had passed. He had been taking truckloads of stuff to donation drop-offs already that morning. I told him I wanted to go through things; I didn't want things thrown out. I wanted to make sure I could get anything that was important to me as a child. I didn't understand why he wanted to do that the very next day, but I had seen him do it on two other occasions. Once when his brother had committed suicide, and the other when his mom passed. Everything had to be thrown out both times. I guess it was his way of going through his own grieving process. My stepdad really loved Mom, and they had been married for so long I actually knew him longer than my own father. I knew he was dealing with his own struggles in processing the loss. When I got to their house and began boxing things up, he asked me to clear out. I didn't expect to have to do it so soon. As I was wrapping a piece of china, Mom came in and said, "I want you to ask him about the rings that I would wear every day. I told him I wanted you to have those rings. Do it right now."

I went into the room where my stepfather was working on boxes, and I asked him about the rings she would wear every day. He acted like he was confused about one of them but then ended up giving them to me. There were two rings. One was given to my grandmother by my grandfather for their fiftieth anniversary. The other was a ring that Mom bought when she first started working. It had a giant smoky topaz. Mom told me that my stepfather had bagged up all of the gold pieces that were in her jewelry box that belonged to my grandmother, and he separated them off so he could take them to a place and sell them. I knew my stepfather loved coins, and I had seen how crazy he got when it came to them—and gold and silver of any kind, for that matter. I never thought he would have taken the pieces, though. She pointed to a tall jewelry box that was next to the door. "You tell him that you want that jewelry box to put your crystals in."

I did as she said and told my stepfather, "I'd like to have that jewelry box. It's by the door, and I want it to put my crystals in."

"Okay, but there's a bunch of junk jewelry in it you probably don't want. It's just a bunch of stuff from Dillard's or Macy's," he said.

Mom said, "Tell him you'll sort it out later. Have Zach load it up into the car now." We were in a Nissan Pathfinder, and it was already packed. *Where are we going to put the jewelry box?* I wondered. "You make room for it," she said. So I had Zach get into the car, and I laid the jewelry box across his lap. It was about three and a half feet tall, and the vehicle was completely loaded down with stuff. I barely had room for Zach and Breezy to ride in the vehicle. When we finally got home, we pulled the jewelry box out, and Zach carried it to the center of the den and set it down.

"Okay, Mom, what do I do with it?" I asked.

She came in. "Open the second drawer and put your hand to the far back," she instructed.

I opened the second drawer and pulled it all the way out to find a silver bracelet covered in bells in the back of the drawer. She said it was a bracelet she wore when she was a little girl and told me it was sterling silver. Then she told me to go to the bottom drawer and look in the far back. As I pulled the drawer out and pushed through the earrings to get to the back, I saw a men's ring with a large garnet stone. "What is this, Mom?"

"It's your grandfather's wedding ring. Your daddy's dad."

Yes, that all made sense. I had received a couple of pieces of jewelry from Grammy when she passed, and they all had garnet and rubies. Giving garnet and rubies was their love language to each other. My dad's parents loved each other very much, and you could tell that in everything they did for each other, in every picture, and it came through even in the stories my dad would tell.

The next day we continued to clean the house, helping my stepdad gather everything. So many things went to donation, even videos of my siblings and me as kids. I wish I could've seen everything before it went.

When the day of Mom's funeral arrived, I didn't know how I was going to drive to the funeral home. It was the farthest place I had been in years. I had Breezy drive, and I rode in the passenger seat. We stopped to pick my stepfather up. I knew he hadn't slept in days and was running on nervous energy. I didn't want him to risk an accident making the drive.

As soon as I walked through the doors of the funeral home, I felt a rush of spirits who had not gone to the light come toward me. It felt as if I were breaking through a banner on a football field. I had to ignore them, as I wanted to be present at that moment for Mom. I'd put together a slideshow with music and pictures I had compiled from her life. I'd written down a few words I wanted to say. The priest had offered to read it, but I knew I needed to be the one to deliver it. My brother and sister sat in the front row. They each had a paper in hand, as they had written some things too. I got up and looked at all the faces of people who I'd met over the years, either because they were members of the family or because they were members of organizations Mom was a part of. I stood there in truth as I looked to the right where my mother's coffin was lying open with red and white roses draped across it. I saw Mom appear next to me just like she would've done in the physical realm. I began by trying to read the eulogy that I had prepared, but instead, all I could do was channel right there at the moment. I channeled the whole thing. Mom even added in some bits. She had me share good things, calling on people to remind them about things they had done together and funny things that had happened, and by the end of my words, I saw and felt a shift within my energy field. I saw Mom happy—she was so happy.

My brother then got up and read one of the funniest eulogies I've ever heard, all of which was true. My sister had handed her words to the priest, and he read them for her. By the end of the ceremony, Mom was standing with my stepdad, trying to comfort him.

I stood out in the parking lot and spoke with family members I hadn't seen in a while, many of whom I had not seen because they thought I was strange. The only cousin who treated me normally and didn't look at me with a judgmental gaze was Todd. He's gay and has such a great love for people and animals. I love him and his husband, and so do my kids. When Mom was alive, she had been worried about Todd since some of his Facebook posts made it seem as if he didn't believe in heaven. I knew from my own personal experiences that sometimes things people go through growing up could lead them to believe that no one's really there on the other side. Before her passing, Mom had said when she crossed over that she was going to visit Todd and tell him there was a heaven and let him know she was happy on the other side. During the funeral, I was so grateful to have Todd and his husband there. It was nice seeing their faces because they offered so much comfort. In the parking lot, Todd told me that he'd had a dream the night before the funeral where Mom came to him. She was wearing a white jumpsuit, and she looked fantastic. He also noted that my father was with her. I smiled and said, "That's exactly what she said she was going to do; she said she was going to visit you."

During that week, I was trying to process Mom's passing, but I had a few clients who I had been working with for years who were very demanding. They didn't seem to understand that I'd lost my mother and needed some time for myself. One of them went so far as to say that if they didn't hear from me, they were going to jump on a plane and come to Texas. Most of my clients understood, though. There were two who had become friends of mine; one was Veronica, who lived close by, and one was Mike from Utah. After hearing the news of Mom's passing, Veronica brought over groceries and cards for the children, letting us know how much she loved us. It meant so much to me—it was so much more than groceries and the cards—it was the fact that she came over and hugged me. It was what I needed. Utah Mike called and said, "If there's anything you guys need, any money, please let me know." He lived far away, but he was one of the friends I felt was truly there for me. He listened and just genuinely cared about what I was going through. I had other friends reach out and ask if there was something they could do. What I really needed was for them to drive over and hug me and not say a word—not give me anything, just hug me. I felt very alone. I had spent so many years comforting people, yet I could only see Breezy and Zach standing before me. I felt like I knew so much about the spirit world and yet knew nothing at the same time.

I needed a call with Belinda Smart. When I spoke to her, I explained that I'd lost my mom and needed to finish clearing any shadow side that was left from any hurt I held onto. It had been a while since I had any sessions with Belinda. She could tell I'd been doing energy work. I think she could see a lot more changes in my energy field than she had seen prior. It felt good being able to reconnect with her again. My biggest obstacle at that point was continuing to remind myself that everything happening was important and not to question it or be angry. I just needed to allow everything to unfold.

Chapter Eleven

The Last Straw

It was the summer of 2019, and it'd only been a few months since Mom had passed. Many of my major clients were based in New York, and they worked in just about every career field imaginable. One day, I had been in the middle of a reading with someone I'll call Liberty. I got a vision of the streets of New York empty and saw what looked like the National Guard. I then saw body bags and trucks. The frequency simply said, "Virus." Liberty was a first responder during 9/11, and when I saw the vision during the reading, I told her. She thanked me for the information and told me she would go to the store and get enough supplies for a couple of months. I'd been reading for her for four years already, and most of the readings were work-related. Liberty knew when I saw something, she could bank on that vision.

When our session was over, I realized I was running late for the next session with another client, Debbie. Debbie was a well-to-do career woman who worked her way to the top in one of the most prestigious companies known worldwide. She lived in Connecticut. I had been reading for her for nine years. Debbie called, and her voice was excited after a day of shopping. We greeted each other as normal, then she asked what I saw for her in the spring of 2020. As I began to look in, I saw several businesses closing their doors—not permanently, but temporarily. As I read for her, I had a vision where I saw people panic buying. *Okay*, I thought to myself, *I just read for Liberty and saw what was happening in New York in the upcoming months. Now, I'm on the phone with Debbie, and it doesn't look any better.* My voice trembled a little as I remembered previous readings where I had told her both good things and bad, but this one was different. "Debbie, as soon as I looked at the timeframe you gave me, the guides showed me some of the businesses around your place are going to be closing temporarily, then they'll be opening up. There's something going on. I read for another person this morning located in New York, and that reading didn't look good either."

Debbie immediately went into fear mode. I could hear it in her voice, though she sounded firm when she said, "You sound completely crazy. You've been reading for me for nine years, and this is the first time you've ever said anything that insane."

I told her, "I'm telling you this so you can get a few extra things. I know you only shop once a week, and I think you need to get a few extra items to have on hand."

Debbie was livid at that point and said, "Do you have any idea where I live? I live in a very wealthy area. Nothing ever closes here; there's so much money."

I softly spoke and said, "There's a virus that will be closing everything down."

She yelled, "I gotta go," and the phone went dead.

After I got off the phone with Debbie, I told Breezy what I'd seen in the New York vision and the Connecticut vision. Breezy got wide-eyed as I shared what had been shown to me. I reminded her what I saw in the vision I'd had earlier in the year when Mom asked about 2020.

Perhaps I was a little disappointed in myself. I never sat around and looked at what was coming up in the world. I felt like I didn't have the luxury of tuning in other than for work. I only focused on what my clients needed, working seven days a week. I didn't even watch the news. I was too exhausted from looking at things for other people to look at anything for myself. I always knew God would bring in what I needed when I needed it.

It was December 30, 2019, and I needed a new car. I wasn't as particular about the type of car as I was about the interior. I wanted an all-white interior; tan-white was not going to work. I went over to the local BMW dealership. When I pulled up, it wasn't but a few seconds before a salesman came out to greet us. His name was Kendrick, and he had a beautiful green energy about him. I told him I was looking for an SUV with an all-white interior. He explained that those are usually special orders, so it wasn't something they normally keep on hand. "Maybe I could show you something else? I have something that's a very light tan," he said.

I had a good feeling that I was going to get the car I wanted that day, and as soon as I had that thought, he said, "Let me run in and check our inventory. I'll be right back." When he came back, he scratched his head with a big smile on his face and said, "You wouldn't believe this. We just got a car like the one you wanted, and it's around back. It's not even listed to go out yet." He walked us behind the dealership, and there sat a beautiful dark-blue BMW. He opened up the door to that car and revealed an all-white interior. While we all stood there looking in at the blinding white interior, I felt that I'd been given a gift from God. It was what I was looking for; it even had a panoramic sunroof. "I'll take it," I said.

"Don't you want to test drive it first?" he said with a laugh. "We will have to get the car ready, and you'll be able to pick it up tomorrow.

Until then, we're not going to let you leave here without a vehicle, so I'll put you in another one just like yours, except it's black."

I got in the rental, and it was beautiful—but not as beautiful as the one I had waiting for me. I thought for a moment, *What would Mom say about this car?* On the way home, Mom's spirit came in. She smiled and said, "I love your new car," then faded away.

When I got home, I had several messages from a woman named Paige McDurk. Paige was frantic and had gotten my number from my friend Carmen. I called her back, and as I did, her spirit guides came in and said, "It's not what she thinks." Upon answering the phone, she told me that her husband, Donald, had been getting home from work earlier than her. She proceeded to tell me that each day when she came home, she noticed the washer running with only the pants, underwear, and socks he had worn that day. "I think he's cheating on me," she said as she began to cry.

A vision of her husband Donald at his workplace opened up in front of me. I saw him walking into the restroom, and when a coworker walked in, regardless of what they were there to do, he would run out. The spirit guides showed me that he'd developed a bathroom phobia as a child when his mom would barge in on him while he was using the restroom. His mother would do that thinking she was keeping him from masturbating, but instead, she was implanting fear that he couldn't let go of. Because of that, he was holding in his bowel movements so he could avoid using the bathroom at work because he was terrified someone would walk in. When Paige called me, her husband had become unable to hold in his bowel movements, and it had been coming out in his pants. When I relayed this to Paige, she sat silently and finally said, "This all makes sense; he had told me how she would walk in on him at random times."

"This needs to be cleared," I said. "The first thing you're going to do is talk to him. Then I want you to tell him you love him and that you've been concerned he's cheating on you. When he's ready, we can clear the fear template that was placed on him from his young teen years."

***

My best friend, who I'd met in one of C.J.'s classes, had asked me to officiate her wedding. The ceremony was set for February 2, 2020. I was thrilled to officiate. I even channeled a special message to say during the ceremony. Breezy and I headed out earlier in the day because the venue was farther than I usually needed to travel, and we thought we could shop on that side of town before the wedding. We had a great lunch and decided to check out one more store before heading to the venue where the wedding was being held. As we were standing in line to check out, my eyes directed my attention to a woman softly coughing. It was just a small cough; it sounded as if she had a tickle in her throat. With my human thinking, I didn't think it was a big deal. Then the frequency came in and said, "She's coughing; you need to notice her energy." At that point, I was sure I was supposed to take notice of the color of the energy field around her. Since I was running late, I just chalked it up to a cough and hurried out the door. On the way back from the wedding, I thought about the cough again and about the energy of everyone we encountered throughout the day. The collective consciousness was intense, and I knew that their higher selves all knew something big was about to happen.

It was lunchtime, and Breezy and I needed to pick up lunch and feed the feral cat we'd been taking care of. We left the house, then I realized I was out of cat food. I must've forgotten to replenish my supply. I ran into Target for the food while Breezy sat in the car. I heard the frequency say, "Go to the cleaning aisle." When I got to the cleaning products, there was an abandoned empty basket in front of the Lysol. The sticker that hung above advertised a sale. It read, "Spend $50 on household products and get a $5 gift card." I grabbed a large pack of paper towels, and the rest I spent on cleaning products. As I was ready to leave the aisle, I heard the frequency tell me, "Get three times this amount in cleaning products." I did as I was told, so it took me a little bit longer to check out since there was so much.

After checking out, I went to the car and popped open the trunk. From the front seat, Breezy turned around to see me loading and said, "What are you doing? Why did you buy so much? I thought you were just going to get cat food, but you were in there for forty-five minutes. I would've gone with you." She had been sitting in the car with the windows down because she wouldn't leave the car running while sitting idly for long periods of time. I quickly loaded, glancing at everyone's energy as they walked in and out of Target. Suddenly, I felt very anxious. Over lunch, I explained to Breezy that God had guided me to buy the extra supplies while I was in the store.

"That makes sense," she said. "I was wondering what you were doing last week when we were at Sam's Club. I noticed you bought gloves for prepping food and other items you don't normally buy."

I explained to her, "When the frequency comes across and tells me to buy, I don't ask why; I just know I'm going to need it." God had been guiding me to gather things all along. I remembered some masks I was guided to buy at the end of 2018. I had a couple of boxes of them in my linen closet. I had one box that contained three N95 masks and a pack of one hundred disposable masks. Thinking back, I didn't really know why I was buying them; I just knew I was supposed to have them on hand.

While in meditation that day, I was shown that the items I'd been guided to purchase were for me to be prepared for a virus that was about to impact the entire world. That virus was COVID-19. When I was being guided about the virus, I was also shown that its purpose was for humanity to purge all prejudices. Instead of dividing people, it should have united them—people were supposed to learn to care about one another. Many people may not realize that humanity continues to carry threads from each lifetime. Those threads have deep roots within their soul group and bloodline. The new mindset was to begin returning to the original blueprint of humanity.

The virus attacked the lungs. On a spiritual level, lungs represent self-love. Each individual walking this planet has experienced previous lifetimes as every race and religion available. It was time to clear the old paradigms that had been put into place by man. I knew the vaccines would come out later, and when they did, the group that would be accepting of the vaccines were also the ones wanting to unite and protect others as well as themselves. The issue at hand was not which political party one was a part of, nor was it the devices being debated: masks and vaccines. The issue at hand was not about relegating a viewpoint based on those subjects. Through humanity's experience with the pandemic, the collective consciousness was trying to go through its progression and evolution into a more expanded, elevated, and inclusive mindset. The group that refused the vaccine still had a longer lesson in removing self-hate or hate toward others because it wasn't about the vaccine itself. This hatred would need to be removed completely from their lineage so that beliefs put in place by man no longer overshadowed the importance of others.

Think about the magic trick where there are three cups with a ball under one. When they are mixed up, most people don't realize the ball has rolled to the floor, so audiences remain watching the cup they thought the ball was under. I use this example to illustrate how many may think this is simply about the vaccine, but it's really the leap in consciousness that's at play. The people who can't release the mindset of the old paradigm will need to reincarnate again somewhere else since Earth's new frequency will not be able to support their way of thinking. Earth had begun its ascension prior to the virus, and it is now trying to purify itself of the human imprint that has been left upon it.

Once the virus is under control, there will be a treatment protocol. The next item that needs to be addressed by humanity is the animal consciousness. Before time began, the agreement between humanity and animals was that both would be equal. Animals were not meant to be seen as inferior to humanity; up until now, they've been viewed this way by most of the world. The time is coming for them to be elevated to the level they were meant to be understood. The pain associated with death is due to the threads of the human consciousness attached to the karma humans took on through the slaughtering and mistreatment of animals. It's time for humanity to stop numbing its senses so it can begin to awaken fully. The consumption of meat numbs the senses much like alcohol or marijuana do. That's why people feel sleepy and refer to meat as comfort food. Through what I've channeled, I've learned that when animal products are consumed, the person takes on the suffering that the animal endured during its lifetime to deliver those goods to us. Each generation has taught its kin to continue the cycle, and this is the cycle that must be broken. It's a thread that was never intended to be interwoven into the fibers of humanity. As the Christ consciousness continues to bring the light in through those who have borne witness to the universal plan, these people will initiate the awakening of their brothers and sisters that transcends the animal instincts that were adopted by man from the fallen ones.

***

Zach was trying to get everything he could out of spring break. It was 2020, and it was his junior year. As he was running around trying to find his baseball hat, I asked him where he was going.

"I'm going to the movies with some friends—why do you ask?" he said.

I told him, "School will be closed next week, and you won't be going back."

"What?" he said in shock. "You're wrong; my school doesn't close for anything."

Looking at him seriously, I said, "Okay, but I'm telling you that there will be no school next week." Even Breezy had her doubts.

A few months had gone by since my last call from Debbie. She reached out again, and she was not her jovial self. She began by saying, "I'm sorry, Katharine." There was a long pause. "I'm sorry I acted the way I did. You have to know, what you told me was crazy, and who the hell would have thought shit would *close*? I should have trusted you since you've never guided me wrong."

I told her it was okay and I wasn't upset. She confessed that the night I told her about the virus, she had attended a book club meeting, and after a few glasses of wine, she told them about her reading with me. Debbie said, "Others weighed in about readings that they'd had with various people that were ridiculous—nothing about the virus, but they all had a good laugh. Then once the virus had begun closing places down, some of the book club members wanted your number."

Since 2018, I'd been getting lots of calls about the 2020 election. As the time of the election got closer and closer, I was inundated with a shitstorm of calls about it. It got to a point where every other call I had, someone was asking who was going to win. "Biden," I would tell them over and over again. So many people were asking, I made a YouTube video stating who was going to win and why they were going to win so I could cut down the number of calls I was getting about the election. I explained the course of the human consciousness and why things were changing. I can't remember what the odds were in Vegas of Biden winning, but I had several people calling and asking me so they could place their bets. When I would tell them I saw Biden winning and that the time Trump had served was ready to come to a close, they would cautiously ask, "Are you sure? Because you're the only psychic I've called who has said Biden will win."

In between calls from my regular clients, I was still taking calls on the psychic hotline. I had a lot of good customers there who I enjoyed talking to, and some were fun to read for. There were several "psychics" who would group together on the site and refer customers to each other when they weren't available. I never joined any groups because, in my readings, I'd received guidance that the clients I was supposed to help would come to me. I also knew the psychics' game, and I didn't like the way they shared personal information about customers with each other. I'd learned that some of the biggest psychic sites had a dashboard system in place. The system would show personal information that psychics had gathered from past readings with each customer so other psychics could see it when they read for the same client. That ensured a uniform reading, so if what they saw didn't happen, they could all blame it on the client with a flimsy excuse. Anything read by another reader would appear to be psychically picked up as new information to the client. It was disheartening to know that just about every site offering readings had something like that in place, monitoring the customers' information.

I was ready to walk away from the hotline completely. One of the other psychics I knew on the site had tried to move away from it and began telling her clients to call her on her personal phone. The following week, she was deleted from the site. She completely lost connection with her clients and had no way to tell them what had happened. I didn't want to lose mine, so I needed to wait until I could figure out a way to tell them how to reach me without telling them directly. There were a lot of forms we had to sign to work for the hotline, and the agreements were constantly updated. One of the stipulations was that we couldn't contact our hotline customers directly or give them personal information that would allow them to contact us outside the hotline.

If you asked any of the readers on a site if they kept information on clients, they would say no so they would look authentic. Because of my contract requirements, I couldn't answer the client when they would say something like, "You're the only psychic who's telling me something different." I wanted badly to tell them the truth—that many of the other psychics continued repeating what someone else had already read so they would all seem correct.

Our calls were sometimes monitored, and they were always recorded, though the recordings were deleted after a while. I knew about the recordings because I had a caller who was verbally abusive after a woman he liked rejected him. He complained about her and talked about doing mean things to retaliate. I blocked him, then reported the caller to the customer service of the site, and after investigating my claim, they blocked him too. They would never take the advisor's word about a customer unless there was proof, and in the case I reported, they just went back and listened to the recording of the call.

I had met Debbie on the site. When I first started reading for her, she would say, "You are the only one who tells me that Brian and I will be together. The other psychics told me he would never leave his wife." She didn't know I was the only one truly reading her situation because the rest of them had their "cheat sheet." The others were sharing information, and she had no idea. There were only a few who worked like I did. The most popular psychics were full of crap, and the site knew it, yet they kept them. Sometimes people just wanted to talk to somebody; those callers would have been better off telling a stranger than wasting their money.

The medical professionals that I'd been reading for took the virus very seriously. However, I was consistently getting calls from my other clients as well as random people asking if the virus was real. It was very frustrating because they had no idea about the careers of some of the people I read for. I wished they could understand that when people in the medical field and first responders would call, I would get a flash of their experiences and feel their emotions. I saw bodies being stacked up, and I saw the frustration in the medical community toward those who were selfish and didn't want to protect others.

***

There is a Yiddish adage that says, "Man plans, and God laughs." In my world, I say, "Woman plans, and God teaches."

It was Chinese New Year 2021, and I had so much planned for the day. I had started preparing all the bases needed for the dishes we'd be enjoying as a family that evening. I had broth boiling on the stove and all the veggies cut for our feast. The recipe I was using was a Chinese soup recipe that had been used for thousands of years. Everything was looking great, but while I was cooking, I got a call from my stepdad asking if the plants in my yard were covered. Since I didn't watch the news, I missed storm warnings all the time, so my stepdad would call when something big was happening. I proudly looked over the broth and the amazing job I did cutting the veggies while I casually yelled up to Zach, "Come down and cover the plants." I yelled up the stairs one more time, but since he was taking so long, I thought, *I'll do it myself*.

I slipped on my shoes that were parked by the door and headed out front. I heard the frequency say, "No, go inside." I completely ignored the warning and began covering the gardenias anyway. I heard the frequency again—then I went down face-first to the ground. My shoe had slipped on the fabric I was using to cover the plants because it had somehow blown under my foot as I was walking away. I couldn't move my leg and began to scream for Zach. This time I *really* screamed for Zach; I wasn't just calling him. He was in his room, and when he heard me, he came running outside. My mother suddenly appeared next to me, and I asked her, "Why are you here? Am I going to die?" At that moment, my neighbor, Bryce, came outside because he heard me screaming. He told me to lay where I was and instructed me not to move. Again I asked Mom, "Am I going to die?" because by then, a few other spirits I recognized had gathered. Bryce answered, "No, you're not going to die." He didn't see Mom and thought I was talking to him.

At that point, I asked Zach to hand me my cell phone so I could call 911. I think he was in shock seeing me lying there, unable to move. When the ambulance arrived, I suddenly remembered the food I'd been cooking and all the bok choy and other good veggies waiting to be added to the spread I had planned. As the first responders were taking my vitals, I yelled to Zach, "Turn off the stove and please put up the veggies too." The paramedics loaded me up, and off I went to the hospital.

My anxiety was skyrocketing, and I was feeling every person's energy who had ever been in that ambulance. It was intense. The male paramedic on my left looked at the female paramedic who was asking me a question and said, "We need to do an EKG now."

"Your heart rate is very high, and we think you may be going into cardiac arrest," the woman told me with the calmest voice she could.

"No, I'm not. Watch me as I look out the back window, and it will go down." As I said this, I looked out the window in the back of the ambulance. They were both surprised as my EKG showed things were normal, and my heart rate went down instantly.

She asked, "How did you bring it down so fast?"

As I looked out the window, I focused on God's energy and detached from the energy of all the previous passengers in the ambulance who had been surrounding me. When I got to the hospital, it was divided off with tape and industrial plastic dividers that kept COVID-19 cases on one side and non-COVID cases on the other. I was ushered into a room by the great EMS crew who picked me up. They closed the door and let me know I'd be getting an X-ray shortly.

Right then, Mom appeared again. "Mom," I said, "it seriously freaked me out that you appeared when my nerves were shot from the ride in the ambulance."

Mom explained, "I am here for you; everything's going to be fine. Look, they have the Disney Channel on for you, and I know how much you love the Disney Channel."

After my X-ray, the doctor confirmed that no bones were broken, but I had a muscular injury that would take a while to heal. He told me a nurse would be in to give me something in my IV until I could get the prescription for the pain filled. Mom was standing on my right side, and there were a few spirit guides present too.

As I lay there, I prayed, "God, why did this have to happen? I've avoided being in public only to have to ride in an ambulance and enter a hospital where the virus is present."

Then the frequency came in and said, "Look at the particles in the air." As I looked in the air, I saw nothing different. Then the frequency said, "Look outside the sliding glass door of your room." My eyes gazed beyond the glass and saw extremely small particles of dark orange floating in the air.

The doctor came back with two nurses. One of the nurses put something in the IV, and within three seconds, Mom was gone—I couldn't see her or the spirit guides. As I began to panic, I suddenly realized they were there even though I had no visual on them. Some substances blind people's spiritual sight. Sometimes the effect is temporary, and thankfully in my case, it would be. I knew I'd be able to see the spirit world again once the medication wore off and I was able to clear my energy field. The doctor told me what he'd given me and said the pain would be back soon if I didn't take the prescription he was planning to send me home with. From previous readings for other people, I had learned that the extended use of certain substances would take a long time to clear from the energy field, even after the individual quit using them.

While I was waiting for the medication to wear off in the middle of the night, I remembered what C.J. experienced when she was blanketed and could sense Archangel Michael's presence but couldn't see him. I recognized how difficult that must have been for her and felt the importance of protecting my own field from being blanketed again.

When I got home, my dog, Anakin, needed to check me out, as he knew I was injured. I've always known that Anakin is my former dog, Dexter, reincarnated. I got to the chair with the ottoman and prayed. Anakin and I have always communicated well. He speaks using telepathy. He is very comforting when I need to hear his words of love and acceptance. After he comforted me and sniffed around, he carefully laid his body against my leg. I immediately saw the heart healing flowing from his body to mine and began to relax.

I'll never forget when I first heard Anakin communicate with me. When he was just a puppy, he said, "Don't give me away." We had adopted our Maltese, Padme, from the animal shelter. When she was adopted, she was very underweight, and she was covered in fleas and urine. The night after she was home with us, I noticed the color in her energy field around her nipples was a strange red color, showing hormonal changes. I didn't worry because I had seen that before in human women who were pregnant. As I rested my head on my pillow that night, my mind caught up to what I'd noticed. I sat up in bed, and it sunk in that she was pregnant.

The next morning, I called the vet clinic and explained that I'd just adopted a dog from the shelter and thought she might be pregnant. The vet tech said, "That's unlikely since the shelter aborts pregnancies when they find them in strays." After I insisted on him giving Padme an exam, the vet confirmed the pregnancy—she was pregnant with six puppies. We raised the pups and found them forever homes. I had planned to let all of the puppies be adopted until Anakin told me not to give him away.

***

After a hectic year in 2020, I began to look at my professional career so far. After doing over fifty thousand readings, I realized I had missed out on a lot of fun by working constantly. I had become a workaholic due to having to survive and wanting to provide a good life for Breezy and Zach. It was something I couldn't help; I had worked all my life and didn't know how to slow down.

Until COVID-19, I was so bothered by all the distress and the trauma that humanity was experiencing that I was ready to walk away and do something that would be less stressful and more relaxing. I thought about teaching tap dance or working in a restaurant. My best friend disagreed with me because I was making as much as a doctor each year. She couldn't imagine that after what I'd seen, I was ready to walk away.

When I started doing this, I had wanted to teach people to awaken and to encourage them to want that for themselves so they could be a light in the world, but I felt like I was only reaching a small group of people. I said a prayer and told the kids that, by the end of 2021, if I didn't feel I was being guided to do this anymore, I was going to quit. I wanted to do something that would bring me some joy. I felt like COVID-19 broke me after all the things I'd seen in visions and readings; all the bodies, the misery, the sadness, and the tears. Why would I see all that if I couldn't help? I explained to the kids that I was finishing a book and wanted to get the information out there so others would recognize their own gifts and want to become open to their spiritual path, regardless of what career they were in. Breezy suggested I start a TikTok account so I could teach people everything I knew. I had nothing to lose, and I felt like it was the best way for people to raise their frequency and understand the teachings.

I encountered a few people who were working as psychics who got angry with me online. They'd leave frustrated comments and ask, "Why are you giving this information out? I hold workshops on this stuff—you should be charging!" I told them I could make ten thousand videos and that still wouldn't cover all that I've learned from the spiritual world.

***

As I was breaking down over the phone to Austin about things I'd seen in visions and some of the things I'd seen during the COVID-19 outbreak, he tried to calm me by saying everything would be fine when he was released and we were together. I pleaded with him, asking him to send some energy healing. That was a common thing he would do after he learned distant healing. He was actually amazing at sending the energy, and I knew that was indeed his superpower. He was really excited to learn more about energy work after getting home.

I was hoping to hold on to the information about the twin flame reader a little bit longer, but it all flew out when Austin and I were purging experiences we hadn't told each other about. He said he kind of knew she was telling everyone they had a twin, but he didn't care about any of that, and his love was unwavering regardless of whether twin flames were a factor or not. I knew the twin flame reader was completely off the mark, but there was a lesson in it all. The lesson from it was simple: don't put your life on hold and focus on a partner. People need to focus on being heart-centered and seeing themself as deserving. The alignment with the right person happens when a person begins to release the guilt and shame they've held onto. I like the twin flame reader as a person and suggested to her that she focus on energy work and help people to open in that way rather than the twin flame angle. She had no idea that I'd sent her at least ten clients because they either needed energy work, and she was good at that, or they absolutely insisted on talking with someone who claimed to specialize in twin flame readings. For each and every one of the people I sent to her, she told them that the person they thought was their twin was indeed and that they would be together.

Over the previous six years, I'd continued to fulfill my promise to Austin and sent him everything he needed during his sentence. I sent him over 710 books on spirituality and energy healing during his incarceration, all of which he donated to the prison's library. Prisoners would find him in the yard or on the job he was assigned there, and they would thank him for the books. On the inside of every cover was written the name "Major." They would share stories about their own awakening and the changes that were happening in their lives after reading the books he'd donated and learning from him during his time there. Major Austin managed to start an unofficial healing group and small class at the prison before he was moved to work release. He was blessed by the wonderful people God sent along his path. Even when he thought he was forgotten, it turned out he was remembered.

***

After my injury, I had to do a lot of physical therapy and go to many chiropractic appointments. One day in June 2021, after coming home from a chiropractic appointment, I began thinking about all I had experienced. I heard the frequency say, "As you're on your path and doing what you are here to do, whatever you ask for will come to you." I thought back to all the times I needed something, and God brought it through to me. All I had to do was think about it, and somehow that item would find its way to me. The things brought to me were not always physical items; oftentimes, they were experiences. Experiencing what I had to in order to learn was tough. However, I could clearly understand the things I needed to experience without human lies or misinformation to cloud my perception. The dance recital where I first saw someone leave their body, the anxiety that was so bad I had to dig deep and find out why, and the witnessing of many people who each had something to share or teach were all orchestrated by the Divine. I was even guided at times, like when I worked at the burger joint and was told by the frequency to clean the bathroom, and lo and behold, I found a ring. The ring wasn't important to me until I needed money to pay for my cat's surgery. I remembered being led to meet Standing Eagle, who taught me about the four directions and herbal medicine, and Marty, wherever she may be, who introduced me to energy work. Then Belinda Smart, who had been a constant throughout my spiritual growth, helped me to understand enough to keep going. The most interesting and rewarding experiences were the times I worked with my amazing clients who came in with situations that I learned from by reading for them. Through reading for some of my clients, I was able to gain a greater view of celebrities and the pedestal they have been placed on by everyday people, only to find that they, too, are in search of their path to happiness. Having never actually been to the Oscars, I have been able to see and feel what the experience is like to go. I've felt the wind in my hair sitting on a yacht off the coast of Ibiza even though I've never physically been there. While reading for a client, I've been able to experience some wonderful things that I couldn't afford the privilege to do in the real world. I was also able to feel the emotions that were connected to various lifestyles. To experience emotions that don't have common adjectives to describe them is a privilege I do not take lightly.

During this incredible journey of finding my superpowers, I encountered a multitude of spiritual beings guiding me, such as Mother Mary, Jesus, archangels, ascended masters, and other universal spirits.

I have not given all the explicit details of those encounters in this memoir, but I intend to do so in future books. I am grateful for all the experiences—the good and the bad—because all of them were necessary steps for me to find my superpowers.

Chapter Twelve

About the Author

Award-winning and bestselling author **Katharine Branham** is a world-renowned psychic medium and remote viewer, having conducted over 100,000 intuitive readings. With a thriving practice in The Woodlands, Texas, Katharine is known for her raw honesty, spiritual depth, and ability to channel profound insights that guide others toward healing, truth, and transformation.

Her debut memoir, *How I Found My Superpowers* (2021), takes readers on a riveting journey of awakening, as she learns to embrace her psychic gifts and encounters powerful spiritual avatars along the way. Following its success, Katharine released a powerful workbook titled "Starting with a Clean Slate." A powerful workbook designed to help readers clear their energy field of judgment, self-sabotage, and emotional blockages. Her newest release, *The Root of Everything*, empowers readers to realign their energy and begin awakening.

Always pushing boundaries, Katharine's third book, *It Was Murder*, dives into chilling true stories of spirit encounters with victims of unsolved crimes—wronged souls whose truths demand to be told. You will want to check out *Sierra Delmar*, a gripping paranormal thriller that blends psychic phenomena with supernatural suspense.

Readers have called it "one of a kind" and a "must-read" for fans of spiritual mysteries. In her latest book, The Root of Everything, is encoded like all her other books with a frequency that helps the reader awaken and open to their highest and best life.

In addition to her writing, Katharine is a devoted animal rights activist and a proud vegan, sharing her home with six beloved pets. When she's not connecting with the spirit world, she enjoys gardening, dancing, and living in harmony with nature.

To explore her books, follow her journey, or book a session, visit: www.katharinebranham.com

www.ingramcontent.com/pod-product-compliance
Lightning Source LLC
Chambersburg PA
CBHW071413070526
44578CB00003B/571